Reiki Raja Yoga

Reiki Raja Yoga

PHILOSOPHY AND PRACTICE
OF HOLISTIC HEALING AND
SELF-REALIZATION

* * *

Grandmaster Shailesh

Feedback about this book can be e-mailed to services@divineheartcenter.com.

Copyright © 2015 by Grandmaster Shailesh
All rights reserved. No part of this publication may be reproduced, distributed, or transmitted in any form or by any means, including photocopying, recording, or other electronic or mechanical methods, without the prior written permission of the author, except in the case of brief quotations embodied in critical reviews and certain other noncommercial uses permitted by copyright law. For permission requests, e-mail services@divineheartcenter.com.

ISBN: 1517384583
ISBN 13: 9781517384586

This book is dedicated to the Holy Absolute, my guru, Meera, and Kailash.

Thanks to Parul, Rajat, Vineet, Gaurav, Sunita, Ruchi, Meredith, and all the initiates of the Divine Heart Center.

Contents

Chapter 1	Introduction	1
Chapter 2	My Divine Realization Journey	10
Chapter 3	Helping You Achieve Holistic Happiness through Reiki Raja-Yoga	18
	Understanding Your Spiritual Self: Eliminating Your Ego	28
	The Principle of Personal Energy Management	37
Chapter 4	The Spiritual Noumena	46
	A Peek into Your Heart	49
Chapter 5	Karma, Samskaras, Sankalpas, and Avidya	62
	Karma	62
	Samskaras	71
	Sankalpas	74
	Avidya	75
Chapter 6	The Aura and the Chakras	78
	Understanding the Chakras	88
	A Brief Look at the Seven Chakras	94
	The Concept of Life-Force Energy	118
	Bija Mantras	127
	The Power of Unconditional Love or Prema	129
Chapter 7	Awakening the Kundalini Energy	132
	Signs of Kundalini Awakening	136

Chapter 8	The Power of Unconditional Love or Reiki · · · · · · · · · · 137
	Benefits That Reiki Can Offer · · · · · · · · · · · · · · · · 145
	A Typical Reiki Treatment · · · · · · · · · · · · · · · · · · 146
	Reiki and the Psychosomatic Connection · · · · · · · 150
	A Brief History of Reiki · 154
	Mention of Reiki in the Ancient Indian Texts · · · · · 157
	The Principles of Reiki · 158
	The Three Pillars of Reiki · · · · · · · · · · · · · · · · · · 162
	The Three Laws of Reiki · · · · · · · · · · · · · · · · · · · 162
	A Mantra to Meditate Upon · · · · · · · · · · · · · · · · 164
	The Attunement Process · · · · · · · · · · · · · · · · · · 165
	The Levels in Reiki · 168
	Reiki—Crystals, Intentions, and Clothing · · · · · · · · 175
	A Reminder about Spiritual Basics · · · · · · · · · · · · 177
	The Process of Healing · · · · · · · · · · · · · · · · · · · 179
	Healing Your Own Self through Reiki or Unconditional Love · 181
	Healing Others through Selfless Love · · · · · · · · · · 183
	You Are the Transformation · · · · · · · · · · · · · · · · 189
Chapter 9	Raja-Yoga · 190
	The Samkhya Philosophy · · · · · · · · · · · · · · · · · · 195
	The Eight Steps of Raja-Yoga · · · · · · · · · · · · · · · 198
Chapter 10	The Crème de la Crème of Raja-Yoga: Kriya Yoga · · · · · · · · · · · · · · · · 214
Chapter 11	Integrating Reiki and Raja-Yoga · 218
Chapter 12	A Note about the Guru-Disciple Relationship · 227
Chapter 13	Yantras or Instruments of Energy · · · · · · · · · · · · · · · 235
Chapter 14	Putting It All into Practice · · · · · · · · · · · · · · · · · · · 238
	Glossary · 245

"I was at a crucial intersection and imbalance in my life with my family and profession when I initiated into the practice of Reiki raja-yoga under the close guidance of Shailesh. My yearlong journey powered by healing and balancing energies has begun. It has shown me clarity and confidence that I look to sustain with self to be an effective person as a husband, father, and colleague."

—*Forty-nine-year-old father of four children and an executive at the Harvard Medical Institutions*

"The nine years' journey on this path has been amazing, and my environment kept getting better and better. Life kept becoming simpler and simpler. Today I do not have any complexities.

"As I continue my journey, I feel an assurance/subtle confidence that the Divine is looking out for me. This faith did not develop overnight, but developed by observing subtle events and changes that took place in my life. Now I am living and enjoying the present moment, rather than worrying about the future or regretting about the past.

"The techniques that are taught at Divine Heart Center can easily be integrated with one's life. I thank Divine every day for putting me on this path. It is a perfect combination of attaining permanent happiness while performing all your existing daily life chores in parallel."

—*VP at a Financial Services company and a father of two children*

"With Reiki in my life and with the guidance of Divine...I was really able to get a better understanding of self, my mind, how I interacted with the universe, and how at peace I was with myself.

"By practicing my Reiki learnings, I find myself not stressing out about work or personal life. I find it easier to believe "the best will happen." I know in my heart that I will *never* be left alone by Divine come what may. So with that confidence in my heart, I take on each day."

—*Relationship manager at a consulting company and a mother*

"In the short span of less than two years of my initiation, I have seen myself grow into a different person. I have observed a lot of behavioral changes in myself. There is subtle happiness that I'm surrounded by (it's not there always, but when it is there, I'm thankful to Divine). My long journey has just started, and I have a guide (DHC guru) on my side, who is navigating me to reach my destination (Divine goal) in a vehicle (DHC techniques) that I need to drive (practice) with patience and endurance and fuel with faith. I do not expect to see the destination right away, but I have faith in my guide, who will keep me on track as he has already completed this journey and is aware of all the pitfalls, from which he will save me."

—*A busy professional and father of two children*

CHAPTER 1

Introduction

* * *

I HAVE BEEN ASKED FOR years about the nature of Reiki raja-yoga. What is Reiki raja-yoga? Is it different from traditional Reiki? Is it similar to Yoga? What benefits can it offer that a seeker cannot gain through conventional practice? How does it help one achieve holistic happiness? And what is self-realization?

Most people have their personal definition of happiness. However, most are either not familiar with or do not completely understand the entire concept of self-realization.

Before I take you on an insightful journey to understand the philosophy and practice of Reiki raja-yoga, it will be worthwhile to point out that I have presented a glossary at the back of the book. The glossary will offer definitions of words that may be unfamiliar to many readers. Such words have been italicized on their first usage as an indicator that they are in the glossary.

Let me begin this book with a quote from Sri Yukteshwar Giri, who was a self-realized guru, an upright Kriya yogi, and a Vedic astrologer: "Everything in the future will improve if you are making a spiritual effort now."

In almost every era, spiritual seekers, as well as scientists, persevere to uncover the mysteries of the human consciousness. We are living in a spiritually meaningful era. We have left behind the era of the "survival of the fittest." We have just passed the era of the "survival of the wisest." The era of the "survival of the most spiritual" has begun. In this era, human consciousness needs to be unraveled with an unprecedented intensity for the greater good of everyone.

The time has come now when humankind can understand its **true potential and power** by being receptive to the guidance being provided by evolved souls who are accessible to humankind today. These evolved souls—the *avadhoots* and the *avatars*—are enlightened beings who have the power to transform human experiences based on their direct experiences of God. They have graduated from the lessons of earth and now work for the service of humankind as guides for humanity's evolution.

They have been directed by the Divine to teach people to tap into inexhaustible healing power, the infinite spiritual field that is present everywhere. The teachings of such masters empower people to achieve holistic happiness.

I have had the humbling privilege of teaching and channeling healing to thousands of people through the ancient yet eternally applicable meditation techniques that were passed on to me by my guru as well as through my direct experiences of God.

Culturally I have my roots in India and consider myself fortunate to have received guidance from some of the finest spiritual gurus. The spiritual techniques that I channel are a result of my highest spiritual experiences bestowed upon me by divine grace merged with the grounded realities of a modern life. With Divine Heart Center's approval, I have made an effort to customize the demanding and powerful spiritual techniques to fit the busiest of lifestyles.

As I begin to write this book, I am reminded of Mother Teresa. As a Roman Catholic religious sister, Mother Teresa made significant contributions to the upliftment of humanity. She mentions how one's healing spirit is more powerful than any darkness that one may encounter.

> There is a light in this world, a healing spirit more powerful than any darkness we may encounter. We sometimes lose sight of this force when there is suffering, too much pain. Then suddenly, the spirit will emerge through the lives of ordinary people who hear a call and answer in extraordinary ways.

I am also reminded of a quote from the Vedic scripture *Maha Upanishad: Vasudhaiva Kutumbakam*:

> *Ayam bandhurayam neti ganana laghuchetasam udaracharitanam tu vasudhaiva kutumbakam.*

This translates to "Only men with a narrow outlook can discriminate by saying: one is a relative; the other is a stranger. For the magnanimous, the entire world constitutes but a family." This statement teaches us that the entire world has to live like one family.

It is a common experience that if one member of a family is undergoing suffering, then the entire family's experience of peace and happiness suffers. One cannot be completely happy unless one's entire family is happy. And if this world is a family, we have to think about spreading happiness in the world for us to find ultimate happiness for ourselves.

I have also experienced that if one is not feeling happy from inside, one cannot make others happy. At some point in time, that inner unhappiness will manifest outwardly and will cause unhappiness to others.

So, therefore, in order to find holistic happiness, we need to find happiness within ourselves and then spread it to our immediate relatives, friends, and acquaintances. We then need to keep expanding our circle of happiness to our community, our region, our nation, and this entire world.

The reason we should do this is because the world is but one family.

The Vedic quote also signifies that you as an individual can participate in the process of healing not only your own self but this world as well.

This is where my mission and the purpose of my life come in: "To create happiness within my world and worldwide through self-healing and self-realization."

This is not just my mission. **I want this to be your mission as well. This mission and the process behind it can transform and heal your life from the inside out.**

Every transformation process depends on a power to operate.

In the path of Reiki raja-yoga, there are two powers of the One Absolute that make transformation to holistic happiness possible: *the power of devotion* (bhakti) *and the power of will* (shakti).

These two powers when tapped into can transform your body, mind, soul, and heart to an extent that you not only experience love and holistic happiness, but also become a messenger of love and happiness.

When the holistic happiness you start experiencing becomes permanent, it is called the state of eternal happiness or eternal joy. This state brings you the first direct experience of the Absolute and begins your journey into self-realization.

Isn't that wonderful?

This path also recognizes the interconnectedness between your personal energy and the energy of the universe—and effective use of this energy system lays the foundation of the transformation to holistic happiness.

There is a much loved and worshipped deity in India who is the true embodiment of the power of devotion and the power of will. This deity is Lord Hanuman. People praise the selfless exploits of Hanuman and his utmost devotion to Lord Rama by singing verses from Tulasi Das's version of the *Ramayana*. Some of the most popular tales mention how Hanuman leaped across the ocean to Lanka, how he single-handedly destroyed Lanka, much to the dismay of the cruel Ravana, and how he flew holding the mountain that had the medicinal root to cure the mortally wounded Lakshmana.

Hanuman is the perfect combination of *shakti* and *bhakti*. Therefore, he is often referred to as the *mahavir* or the greatest warrior.

Almost everybody struggles to find happiness. Those who discover holistic happiness while also making progress into self-realization become mahavir or the strongest warriors and yogis.

This path can also be called the path of divine grace and divine will. Devotion attracts divine grace. Similarly, by exercising our own will in a positive way, we harness the unlimited power of the divine will.

The path of Reiki raja-yoga combines meditation techniques to generate devotion in your heart and inculcate a strong positive willpower in your mind.

A heart full of love and a mind full of power can ensure that *you have the power to create soul-healing miracles that can enable you to achieve holistic happiness.* This path guides you to skillfully and effortlessly maneuver the two powers of the One Absolute into your life.

Holistic happiness is a subjective term. What one person needs to experience happiness is very different from what another person needs. However, **everyone wants to be happy**.

This path allows you to define and find your own holistic happiness. You may find inner happiness more important than happiness found through external accomplishments. Or, most likely, you are at a point in life where there are many worldly achievements that you want to make before you can call yourself happy. This path supports both pursuits—the pursuit of happiness through worthwhile outer achievements as well as the pursuit of inner happiness irrespective of outward circumstances. This path supports your pursuit of holistic happiness based on **your** definition of holistic happiness!

This path also respects that holistic happiness is the foundation for the pursuit of self-realization. You cannot find the Absolute when you are unhappy in your current state of affairs. For example, if you are going through a relationship crisis, it is almost impossible for you to focus on meditating on the Absolute until you address the relationship matter at hand. In fact, constantly thinking negatively about that toxic relationship even in your meditation will make the situation more difficult instead of resolving it.

Eternal happiness in the Absolute is founded on holistic happiness in the realm of relativity.

There are specific steps that one can take in order to discover holistic happiness. You will discover those steps and the path as you read through the book.

As Lahiri Mahasaya, the Yogi Christ of India, rightly mentioned, "*Divine union is possible through self-effort, and is not dependent on theological beliefs or on the arbitrary will of a 'Cosmic Dictator.'*"

There is self-effort required to achieve holistic happiness. Simply put, you need to *eliminate your personal, self-created energy blocks and understand yourself.*

In order to do this, you need to develop a deeper understanding of yourself.

Do you understand yourself completely?

Do you wear a mask or label? This could be your name, your position, your physical body…anything. We will talk more about this as we discover the difference between our true selves and our egos in the coming chapters.

How can you eradicate these personal, self-created energy blocks?

There is a specific technique that can link you to the unblocked and infinitely potent spiritual field. This spiritual field can help you dissolve and burn your energy blocks, also called karmic blocks, using the power of divine grace and will.

Once you melt or dissolve your karmic blocks, you attract holistic happiness, and you speed up the process of your spiritual evolution. The ultimate state of spiritual evolution is *sat-chit-ananda*, which means "conscious existence in eternal bliss."

Sat means eternal consciousness. It is the essence of life or the "livingness" that is present in you. You *are* alive.

Chit means the peaceful, complete, and unbroken awareness of this consciousness. You *realize* that you are life itself (not just John or Mary).

Ananda means pure bliss. The essence of life is bliss. *The realization that you are life itself is bliss.*

The nature of the Absolute is *sat-chit-ananda*. The seeker starts with oscillating states of happiness and sorrow. After practicing Reiki raja-yoga, a more stable state of outer and inner happiness is achieved. After years of regular practice, holistic happiness manifests in the initiate's life. With further self-effort and surrender, one experiences a state of eternal happiness. On further continuation of the practice, through unflinching faith, surrender, and determined effort, *sat-chit-ananda* is realized.

The zenith of holistic happiness is the realization of *sat-chit-ananda*. The first step, however, is to achieve holistic happiness.

This book will familiarize you with the philosophy and the technique that can help you achieve holistic happiness. This book will also help uncover the greatest mystery surrounding the Absolute. (*Sat-chit-ananda* is also the innate nature of the Absolute or the Creator.)

As you read further, you will learn how Reiki raja-yoga, through its single objective of creating happiness within yourself and the whole world, links science with spirituality and explains the unison among your body, heart, mind, and soul, helping you reach a state of *sat-chit-ananda* or eternal happiness.

Through this book you will be able to gain access to some innovative and practical techniques that will encourage healing on physical, emotional, mental, and spiritual levels.

While this is not a Reiki raja-yoga manual, the basic meditations mentioned in this book will help you get started on your spiritual journey. The knowledge that is provided in this book will aid in your journey to self-discovery, understanding, awareness, personal growth, and spiritual development.

My foremost intent is to take you one step forward in your journey toward holistic happiness.

You will understand the root cause of unhappiness, and I shall introduce you to the concepts of *aura*, *chakras*, *vastu*, and energy, so that you are able to eradicate energy barriers to health, wealth, relationships, and knowledge.

Many healing miracles have been created at the Divine Heart Center by divine grace through myself and other soul-healing servants that I have had the privilege to initiate in order to spread happiness in this world. In order to help you understand this powerful spiritual practice (*sadhna*) that combines the path of self-effort (*shram*) and surrender (*samarpan*) to the Divine, I feel that it is appropriate to give you a few glimpses from my own journey.

CHAPTER 2
My Divine Realization Journey

✴ ✴ ✴

When the absolute reality is known, it is seen to be without
any individual selves, and devoid of any objective forms;

All past [mental and physical] actions that
lead to hell are instantly wiped away.

After the awakening, there is only vast emptiness; this vast
universe of forms ceases to exist [outside of one's self].

Here, one sees neither sin nor bliss, neither loss nor gain.

In the midst of the eternal serenity, no questions arise;

The dust of ignorance that has accumulated
on the unpolished mirror for ages,

Is now, and forever, cleared away in the vision of truth.

— Yung-chia Ta-shih, Zen Buddhist poet and sage

My first spiritual experiences started when I was seven or maybe eight years old. I still remember in the night my astral body would project out of my physical body while I was asleep, and I would find my awareness in my astral body looking down at my sleeping body. This happened on many occasions and sometimes for many nights in a row. Gradually I developed an ability to turn my astral body hovering in midair so that instead of facing the ceiling fan only a few inches away from my astral nose, I could turn around to see my sleeping physical body.

The desire to help the world and an innate sense that there is something beyond this material world was always there. Sometimes in my dreams, I would imagine that I was Superman saving people. The Superman dreams used to be vivid and had a good story line. It was probably a way for my mind to vent out this desire from my previous lives to do something positive and to create an impact at the level of entire humanity. The dream repeated so many times that at one point in time, I could change the events in my dream the way I wished to; I had control over what I was dreaming. This was an amusing discovery for me as a kid—the ability to change the course of the events in my dream while dreaming!

My father was a PhD and a doctor of literature in the English language. My mother had a masters of arts (MA) degree in Hindi. This allowed me access to parents who had a very strong command over the English and Hindi languages and created an innate ability in me to spend hours in research and contemplation. This ability has come in handy in my spiritual pursuits.

My mother was brought up in a highly spiritual environment and knew many of the Sanskrit scriptures by heart. She could spontaneously repeat mantras and shlokas from different scriptures, and her memory continues to amaze me even today. My father didn't believe in God in his earlier life, I am told, but around midpoint in his life, he developed faith in God. At least when I became conscious of my self during my childhood, I found a father who was principled and had reasonable faith in God. My mother, on the other hand, was very religious and used to have visions of saints, deities, and gods.

Once I was traveling in a rickshaw in Agra with her when she told me, "Look! Rishi Vishvamitra is walking there," pointing toward an unpaved side lane. Rishi Vishvamitra was one of the most venerated *rishis* or sages of ancient times in India. He is also credited as the author of most of *mandala* three of the *Rigveda*, including the *Gayatri* mantra. At that time, I was so little that I didn't care who Vishvamitra was and what my mother was saying. Later on as my spiritual vision developed, I found her description to be accurate; she had seen a vision of a rishi with glowing complexion and hair extending from his head to his toes.

Oftentimes when I would enter my parents' bedroom (ours was a modest two-bedroom apartment when I was growing up), I could feel the presence of a huge tiger. At that time I was too busy with my innocence to reason as to why I was seeing or imagining a tiger in such intricate detail when I had never seen a tiger up close at that age. And why did the tiger not scare me but just looked at me with utmost kindness and peace every time I would see it? Later as an adult, I realized one day in a meditation that the vision of the tiger that I had since forgotten was the presence of the Goddess Durga in the room. Her presence has overseen the protection of my family through thick and thin.

A couple years back in a casual conversation, my mother told me that throughout most of her adult life she had been mentally chanting the mantra *"Aum aim hreem kleem chamundaye vichay."*

This *navarna* mantra is the *bija* mantra of all three divine mothers: *Maha Kali*, *Maha Lakshmi*, and *Maha Saraswati*. So it embodies all three mothers. It is considered an ideal mantra for reaching the Divine.

In 2014, after I visited Badrinath and Dwarka in India with a group of my initiates, I was counting the number of *dhams* that I have visited. I realized that I have visited three out of the four *dhams* considered sacred in Hinduism: Rameshwaram, Badrinath, and Dwarka. The one that I have not yet visited (in this life) is Puri. While this thought process was not known to my mother, in a casual conversation over the phone, she told me a story that made me smile. Before my mother was married, she went to visit a Shiva temple in Puri. When she bowed her head in front of the idol of the deity, a garland came from nowhere and fell around her neck. Within a few days after that incident, her marriage got arranged with my father.

I was born on the day of *Teej*. The festival of *Teej* is celebrated in the northern part of India to welcome the monsoon season. It is dedicated to Goddess Parvati and signifies her union with Lord Shiva. Women celebrate *Teej* and remember the goddess. They also pray for longevity and wellness of their husbands and families.

On the day of my birth, my mother was fasting in a fast called the "*nirjala vrat*"; this is a fast in which the seeker doesn't even drink water for twenty-four hours. The waterless fast is considered extremely difficult to follow as the day falls in the hot Indian summer, and thus, it is deemed as very pious austerity. I didn't make things easy for my mother! She told me that she was guided by the goddess to have a third child, while my father didn't feel the need for a third one given that my elder brother and elder sister made a good enough family.

The gist of all this is that the blessings of Mother Kali and an unexplainable attraction toward her have always been there in my life. From her formless presence, I drew my strength and knowledge many times; and like a divine mother, she has stood by me and protected me with her power of time (*kaal-i*) and power to destroy ego and ignorance.

One night—I guess I was approximately nine years young at that time—I stood on the enclosed balcony of our apartment. As I was looking at the sky, I saw a meteor falling from the skies. I had been looking for one for a few nights as my mother had told me that if you ask a wish when you see a meteor, it comes true. I was relieved that night when I saw one in the starry skies, and I asked for *"Brahm"*—the Holy Absolute.

Growing up I did very well academically, and while being part of a middle-class family in India was not easy, my overall childhood and teenage years were good and full of small adventures. The lure of the unknown was always there, and I dabbled in many esoteric practices, much to the dismay of my ever-concerned neighbors (in India your neighbors worry about your future more than your own family does).

I read spiritual books and learned *pranayama*, hypnotism, handwriting analysis, and Divine knows what else all on my own, with, of course, some sanction from my father, who I am sure must have been worried on the inside but never came across as unsupportive of my unusual interests.

During summer vacations I would often spend my time sun gazing or indulging myself in *"tratak"* practice by staring at myself in the mirror for close to an hour—much to the amusement of my sister, who would often comment that these practices were making me lazy.

However, in a middle-class family in India in those years, summer camps were unheard-of, and one had a lot of time at hand to experiment, especially during those *loo* (hot and dry winds)-laden afternoons where one couldn't venture out due to the chances of getting heatstroke.

On some days I would manage to convince my friends to get hypnotized by me, and while they have all become busy professionals today, they did make some very good subjects back then. My partner in crime at that time was my dear friend Anubhav, whom I would hypnotize and then prick with a pushpin; under the influence of hypnotism, he would feel as if he was being touched by a soft rose! It is possible that he was just playing along to bolster my confidence, but my hypnotic skills appeared pretty real those days.

I remember that I would develop an upset stomach during high school when studying in a strict-disciplinarian Catholic school; it was not easy to leave the class without being slightly reprimanded by the teacher. So I discovered a way that would fix my stomach getting upset during school hours. The fix was that I would recite the prayer of "Hail Mary" twenty to thirty times on my way to school. That seemed to do the trick except on days when I would forget. *Karma*!

Agra, my birthplace, with its proximity to Mathura—the birthplace of Lord Krishna—and its history of Mughal rule, is a culturally diverse city. On my way to school, I would leave home listening to the *"bhajans"* that my father would tune into on the radio, and on my way I would pass through a *"dargah"* of a *pir* right by the locality where Neem Karoli Baba lived when he was a householder. I would finally reach my Catholic school and read "Heavenly Father…" All these spiritual inputs blended in my receptive mind and created an appetite to consume more spiritual energy.

Of course, being the son of a professor, the quality of education I and my siblings received was top-notch, and the expectation at home was to excel in academics.

I did well in high school, and that led to my admission in BITS Pilani, a prestigious engineering school in India that I sometimes compare to MIT in Cambridge, Massachusetts—the state that I now call home. The engineering curriculum was demanding and engaging. It shaped my scientific temperament. While I did well in my studies, I temporarily lost touch with my spiritual pursuits for those four years; it was also a time when I was gaining other life experiences, and my prior ad hoc and undisciplined spiritual pursuits were subconsciously arranging themselves for a more meaningful direction and a much bigger discovery.

My ad hoc and unorganized pursuits didn't satisfy my curiosity about the Absolute; they just increased my appetite for the Absolute. It was not until I met my guru, Shri Vijay Bansal, in 1998 that a disciplined approach toward spirituality using the techniques of Reiki developed. My interest in Reiki started as an academic interest; I didn't learn Reiki to fix something wrong in my life but just to learn more and to develop myself.

However, later on as profound spiritual experiences started happening, Reiki and raja-yoga took on a different dimension in my life. *Reiki and raja-yoga became my life and my lifestyle.*

As I progressed, blessings of my gurus from my previous births guided me; direct blessings and visions were received from Shri Param Brahm (the form of the Holy Absolute), Mahavatar Babaji, Yogeshwar Krishna, Lahiri Mahasaya, Shri Yukteshwar, Paramahansa Yogananda, Jesus Christ, Mother Mary, Sai Baba of Shirdi, Guru Hanuman, Guru Ved Vyas, Sensei Usui, Swami Vivekanand, and many other kind gurus. All these experiences have become a part of me and have coalesced into an inner silence but an outer urgency to make something happen—to create a shift in human awareness toward the Absolute, to usher in the era of "*Brahmarthis*"—a generation whose purpose is *Brahm*, the Holy Absolute.

My wife has supported me in this challenging and fruitful journey, which has often meant steering two boats at the same time. Being a

Reiki master herself and being the daughter of my guru, she has the skills to handle a husband who is unconventionally spiritual but also needs to keep his feet grounded on earth for the day-to-day life to run.

All this has happened while maintaining a progressive career in information technology. While working and traveling in many countries, I have assumed many roles as a technologist and a business consultant in some of the top companies in the world. My professional career has allowed me access to some of the best talented technologists and business consultants, whom I have learned a lot from. In parallel, my spiritual anchor has allowed me to stay true to myself and keep expanding internally into the kingdom of the Absolute.

My meditations are *an inexhaustible source of power, which is used partly in the discharge of my worldly duties, which are urgent and demanding; partly in working out the karma of my initiates through my own body, mind, and soul; and partly reinvested in the next stage of my spiritual expansion.* This is all happening *by the grace of the Absolute and the grace of the gurus.*

The journey to connect the material to the spiritual, to connect a life of business with the meaning of life, to bridge that which sells with that which gives liberation has been challenging and rewarding at the same time. By divine will and by divine grace, after many years of external toiling, mental "*Mahabharata,*" and inner soul-searching, a power has emerged—the power of self-realization.

A raja-yogi has manifested, one who is fully present in this world yet intensely engrossed in the Absolute.

From this plane of consciousness, **I offer to serve humanity**.

CHAPTER 3

Helping You Achieve Holistic Happiness through Reiki Raja-Yoga

✻ ✻ ✻

"It is easy for me to plant the seed of love for the Divine in those who are in tune with me." —Paramahansa Yogananda

I am blessed to have a nice herbal garden. And since I observe the process of plant growth very closely and keenly, I must mention that the very fact that I become instrumental in fostering the growth of another living being brings me huge contentment!

Now, plants go through various stages: pollination, fertilization, formation of seeds, dispersal of seeds, germination, growth, flowering, and then pollination again…the cycle continues.

Some of these stages are not visible to the naked eye, but sometimes you get signals. You may notice the formation of buds, the rotation of petals, and then one day, when you are really happy in your garden, you notice the browning of the flower, and then suddenly it droops and falls away.

Ah…You did not want that!

The reason that I am bringing up this story here is owing to its strong connection to the various stages in a human being's life.

We all go through various stages of transition—birth, kindergarten, first day at school, first day at college, first love, first day at job, marriage, change of job, children, parents aging, another job, children leaving home to pursue further studies, death of parents, retirement, career of children, loss of a partner, our own death or fear of death, and finally leaving a legacy through the next generation that we build...

Sometimes it takes years to get prepared for every single transition. At other times it is so fast that you don't even know when it happened.

Now, you have two options: either to resist these transitions, or to accept them and learn to love yourself through every part of the process. A simple understanding that the force that brought you on this planet is still there, guiding you through each and every transition, can make learning to love yourself easier.

Each day of your life, you secretly aspire to achieve one single thing—happiness.

Whether it is your first day at college or your first day at a job, whether it is your parents aging or your partner's birthday, whether it is your retirement or your child's school fund, you strive to achieve one single thing through all these transitions.

That single thing is called holistic happiness.

Let me ask you to do a thirty-second activity. Close your eyes and think about what you want most in life!

Open your eyes and write it down on a piece of paper.

Some of you would have written getting through a difficult exam or job interview, others might have written perfect health for self or loved ones, and yet others might have written name, fame, and money. Irrespective of what you have written on this piece of paper, think about what this one thing would bring into your life.

There is only one answer to this—happiness!

- Perfect health implies happiness.
- Name, fame, and money imply happiness.
- Getting through a difficult job interview implies happiness.

This brings us to a very important conclusion—the truth of life: All human beings by nature strive for holistic happiness. They may not know it, yet they desire it and make efforts to achieve it.

Human beings are really complicated. They process information at all levels and use this information to perform various tasks every day. Think about your own self.

Do you need physical security, financial freedom, power, accomplishment, pleasure, self-expression, a rich emotional life, and then mental and spiritual growth?

Wow…That's a long list…

Who doesn't need these things? With the complexities of life, humans do need help to sort things out. You do want that magic wand that can help you achieve all the above things and, of course, enable you to gain access to that one thing that you did not even mention but are striving for—that thing called happiness.

Let me first mention that happiness is not a chase. It is not something that can be sought directly; it works from the inside out.

If you introspect on your life today, you would notice that you have achieved happiness—in certain areas of your life.

What you are striving for is happiness in all areas of your life.

How can you achieve that?

Well, holistic happiness practically begins by eliminating your personal energy blocks. The best way to do this is through a practice that can connect you to the inexhaustible spiritual field from where you can draw grace and willpower to eliminate these blocks.

Before we delve into this further, let us explore the causes of unhappiness:

Lack of meaning in your day-to-day life

Franklin D. Roosevelt rightly said, "Happiness is not in the mere possession of money; it lies in the joy of achievement, in the thrill of creative effort."

You have a busy nine-to-five work schedule, correct? And this is so mechanical: you get up in the morning, exercise (because you have to and not because you want to), have breakfast (sometimes, when you have time), sip a cup of coffee (if you can afford that luxury), and head out to work. You come back home, exhausted, and either grab a pick-me-up sandwich or prepare a quick dinner for yourself and begin the process of answering your e-mails once again. Two more hours, and you are tired, so you finally doze off.

The question here is, "Did you really intend to spend your life like that?" Did you really want to get so absorbed in work that you have no time for your personal, emotional, and spiritual development?

OBSESSION WITH FUTURE OR PAST
Sometimes you are obsessed about the happenings in your life; you keep thinking about what has happened or what you want to happen.

The mindfulness techniques of Reiki raja-yoga teach you to be aware of the present, to focus on the present and to live in the present.

Helen Keller rightly said: "When one door of happiness closes, another opens, but often we look so long at the closed door that we do not see the one that has been opened for us."

FEELING UNHEALTHY OR OUT OF SHAPE
Now, that's a no-brainer. You cannot stay happy if you are unwell, can you?

UNFAVORABLE COMPARISONS
A number of individuals believe that happiness can only be achieved when they achieve a certain level in life. You eye that corner office of your boss and so much want to take his or her place.

You want to compete with a friend who owns a mansion at the beach. And when you reach that destination, you are still not satisfied—because now, you have a new destination in mind.

Practicing gratitude for the things that you are blessed with can enable you to get rid of your false ego and open your eyes to the world of possibilities.

NEGATIVES...OH MY, MY!
Imagine you meet a colleague from your previous office after a year, and he asks you how it is going for you in the new company. You reply that you are doing well, and this friend of yours tries to dig deep.

So, he suggests a cup of coffee and mentions that you look a little stressed-out. "Is it too much work pressure?"

And there you go...Yes, your boss makes you work too much, he calls you on weekends, he does not pay overtime, and then there is family stress too...you just go on and on...

Your completely positive self suddenly turns negative—without you even noticing the transition.

And it is just in a matter of seconds...*Somebody has been able to barge into your personal space, broken your protective shield, and converted you into a negative person.*

When you stop focusing on the opportunities in your life and the positives that each life situation has to offer you, you become a naturally negative person—an unhappy person. You try to repel happiness subconsciously.

PERSONAL ACCOUNTABILITY, ANGER, AND FEAR OF FAILURE

The spirit is in unlimited spontaneous bliss.

The soul separates from the spirit and is in limited yet spontaneous bliss.

The ego forgets the soul and, hence, forgets the bliss.

This differential in bliss is called anger.

This separation from the spirit causes fear.

Once again, your false ego comes in the way of your happiness here. You subconsciously choose to not take control of your life and let someone else take accountability for the situations in your life.

At other times, in your quest to achieve perfection, you gradually begin the process of sabotaging your future. You start thinking too much and give in to your false ego, the negative emotions, anger, and fear. And because you begin to fear failure, you begin to lose control of your life. You just let go of happiness.

Low self-esteem
Many times we start belittling ourselves or surround ourselves with people who belittle us. Once again, this leads to negativity, a false perception of things, and, of course, unhappiness. We are constantly angry with ourselves, causing pain in our own lives.

As Marcus Aurelius said, *"Very little is needed to make a happy life; it is all within yourself, in your way of thinking."*

Financial debt
Nobody wants to remain in financial debt. And one main cause of financial debt is you not understanding your potential.

When you do not understand what you are capable of, you are not able to make channelized efforts to free yourself from this debt—leading to an unhappy you.

Let me try to explain the causes of unhappiness through a simple analogy—the dishwasher analogy.

The mind of a seeker can be compared to a dishwasher filled with soiled dishes. These soiled dishes represent the fear, the anger, the bitterness, the suffering, and the general disturbance in the seeker's mind. This dirt of ignorance prevents the seeker from achieving sustainable peace and happiness.

All beings desire happiness.

So, what does the seeker try to do?

The seeker tries to acquire and use the water of knowledge to cleanse his or her ignorance and understand the cause of his or her unhappiness. This worldly oriented seeker becomes learned by reading and watching all the books and videos he or she can find and by collecting all the degrees and titles he or she can acquire.

What this seeker needs to remember is that this theoretical knowledge gained from books and videos is just like the water in the dishwasher. Even after running the dishwasher with plain water, the tough grease of unhappiness and mental disturbance does not get eliminated.

To remove these nasty stains of dirt and grime seems to be a mammoth task. It surely appears like a lofty goal, doesn't it?

But it is within your reach. The spiritual tools of Reiki raja-yoga will empower you to live a more fulfilling, loving, satisfying, and spiritually meaningful life.

So, how can you achieve eternal happiness?

Eternal happiness is the highest achievement.

All achievements are a product of our aura—our personal energy field.

We direct this energy through our mind—our mental power.

Spiritually ignorant karma or actions create mental and auric blocks.

These blocks make our love conditional and our happiness impermanent.

Our Divine-directed potent techniques heal these blocks.

The result is progress toward unconditional love and eternal happiness.

The Divine is unconditional love and eternal happiness.

These techniques blend in the busiest lifestyle. Be sincere.

A spiritual person accepts with courage where his or her past karma has placed him or her in life and, without brooding continues to march ahead in the pursuit of holistic happiness. Holistic happiness can also be defined as practical abundance in health, wealth, wisdom, joy, relationships, and spirituality.

In order to make your holistic happiness eternal, you must ensure that a deep pursuit of spirituality is an integral part of your life.

How do we define spirituality?

To me, spirituality is the inclination of a sentient mind such that it desires to know more about itself and in the process begins to find its true identity as the unlimited spirit.

Make sense?

Let me try to simplify this further.

Do you sometimes tell yourself how happy you want to be or how sad you are feeling at the moment? Do you sometimes explain your likes and dislikes to your own self? Do you explain to yourself the next career move you want to make or the sport that you like playing?

We all do that.

The question I have for you is, "Do you understand yourself?"

Who are you?

What do you mean by this single-letter word "I"?

If you do not know yourself, chances are that you do not understand your likes and dislikes completely.

Your happiness directly depends on what you know about yourself.

Not knowing your true identity, you tend to act on the periphery of your mind. Therefore, your decision-making power is limited; it is based on fear or cultural or social conditioning, and eventually you become dis-eased—"not at ease."

Not being at ease with your own self, being bitter from the inside due to the partially happy state that you are in, you tend to spread this unhappiness to people around you.

In the process, you, although unknowingly but, habitually start limiting the happiness of others. The primary reason for this is because you begin to rationalize in your subconscious mind; you are convinced that if you were not able to achieve something, nobody else will be able to.

This limited state of the mind is called the state of *avidya* or ignorance or being nonspiritual. The subtle limiting collective principle in creation that hides your true identity from the mind is called *maya* or cosmic hypnosis or Satan or the measurer (i.e., that which is limited can be measured).

Spirituality is the practice of unfolding yourself layer-by-layer to ultimately realize the inexhaustible spirit overflowing with pure unlimited love and dazzling with infinite intelligence. When you begin to see glimpses of your unlimited and infinite self, you feel less fearful, less stressed, more loving, and frequently happy. And then, you develop the power to spread this happiness around yourself, fostering happiness within your world and worldwide.

UNDERSTANDING YOUR SPIRITUAL SELF: ELIMINATING YOUR EGO

> Like two golden birds perched on the selfsame tree, intimate friends, the ego and the Self dwell in the same body. The former eats the sweet and sour fruits of the tree of life while the latter looks on in detachment. As long as we think we are the ego, we feel attached and fall into sorrow. But realize that you are the Self, the Lord of life, and you will be freed from sorrow. When you realize that you are the Self, supreme source of light, supreme source of love, you transcend the duality of life and enter into the unitive state. —*The Mundaka Upanishad, Chapter 3, Mantra 1-3*

Raja-yoga is also called the "yoga of the mind." A great emphasis is placed on using the mind to objectively observe the world around you and to understand its transitory yet clingy nature. A far greater emphasis is also placed on turning the searchlight of the mind inward to probe into the nature of the ego itself. If you are able to make these inner and outer observations with patience and objectivity, you will understand how our ego creates an incorrect self-image, which then limits our happiness.

So, what is ego?

Ego is the root cause of all unhappiness.

From a psychological perspective, the ego or *ahamkar* can be defined as pride about oneself. Thoughts such as my life, my wealth, my happiness, my body, my mind, or my family all result from one sole thing—the ego.

On a psychological plane, pride, false image of oneself, superiority, and "I"-ness are all connected with ego.

Looking at this from a spiritual angle, the term "ego" would imply considering yourself to be separate from others and the Absolute.

Why does this happen?

This happens because you begin to identify yourself solely with your physical body. You begin to believe that your existence is limited to the power of your five senses, intellect, and mind. So ego is your attachment to an incorrect idea about yourself.

Let us take an example here. You have an image of yourself: you believe that you are an extremely honest person. And one fine day, somebody talks to you about how you lied about certain things.

True, you are honest, but you are also attached to this image—to the extent that if someone tries to prick there, it begins to hurt. So when this somebody gave you an example of a situation where you lied, it began to hurt.

Similarly, you may get attached to various things: you are a perfect wife, a supermom, a great career person, a people's manager…the list can go on and on. This attachment is in a way ego—you get hurt when somebody tries to break this perception or attachment that you have about your own self.

Imagine believing that you are a supermom, and the feedback that you get from your child's school is on your child's casual attitude and misbehavior.

What would be your immediate reaction?

You would begin to think, *How is it possible? I brought him up with so much love and care, I gave him all the great samskaras or values, I spent quality time with him, and he's still casual and misbehaved?*

There you go…The ego (or the attachment to an incorrect image of yourself) has done its job. You are so attached to this image of being a supermom that even the slightest of things hurts.

Do you notice how many times the word "I" comes when you are thinking about this incorrect image of yourself?

Sometimes you may have an incorrect idea about yourself—you may believe that you are a supermom when in reality you are not. And it is all right, because you have loads of other things to manage.

A simple incorrect idea may not be the source of any disturbance. If you have an incorrect idea about yourself but are not attached to that idea, you will not get hurt. The ego will not come into play.

Attachment leads to fear. The moment there is attachment, there will be fear—fear of losing the thing that you are attached to.

Let me take an example of a small valuable object here. Choose any object that you have acquired and are in love with. Try holding that object for some time. How long can you hold that object? A few minutes? A few hours? A few days? A few months?...In the end, it will fall, and you will lose it, won't you?

Now, what will happen when you lose this object?

Obviously you will experience pain—pain because you were so much attached to this object.

Go back now and think about the time that you spent holding the object. What were your emotions at that time? I am sure almost all of you experienced fear—fear of losing that object—and therefore tried to hold on to that object even more tightly. This fear brought pain.

So, while it is acceptable that it pains you when you lose a valuable object, your attachment to that object ensured that you did not enjoy the object and always lived in fear and pain of losing that particular object. Simply imagining the object moving away from you leads to fear and pain.

But you always knew that one day you would lose this object, didn't you?

Yes, and yet the false attachment ensured that the pain you were supposed to get in the future came to you right now!

Why did you get the object in the first place?

You got it because **you wanted to enjoy it, live it, love it**—correct?

And what happened all this time?

You got so much attached to it that instead of enjoyment, you feared losing it, you were stressed-out, and the thought of losing it made you angry. The result? You caused pain to your own self.

So, feelings such as fear, pain, anger, and ego all got created because you were attached to something, knowing that it is temporary.

I now urge you to look at your life. You got a body, you acquired a name, you were blessed with a family, you acquired loads of wealth, you achieved a rocking career, and you acquired a great position… Why?

You got all this so that you could enjoy it during the time you have it.

The natural tendency of humans is to try to protect things because they are attached to them—even when they are aware that these things are temporary.

You are attached to your position, to your wealth, to your property… and in the process, you try to protect these—living each day in fear, stress, and anger, all because of your ego, your *attachment to an incorrect image of something*!

This may impact relationships too. You fear losing your parents, your loved ones, your children, your partners, and deep in your heart you fear death; you fear losing your body. You may call it "your self," but this self is different from your actual self.

So, deep within your heart, you are carrying an incorrect image of your own self; you see yourself as your physical body.

But you always knew that you would die one day, didn't you?

Your physical body is temporary, and yet you live in that fear—all the time.

When you dissociate yourself from ego, you begin to believe in the soul principle; you understand that your true state of existence is identification with the Divine or the soul within you. Therefore, you understand that "you" don't die—only your body dies!

When you are not aware of your true identity, you develop a kind of a spiritual amnesia—you forget who you are and begin to believe that your physical body is you. This forgetfulness leaves you confused.

If we compare a child born today with a child who was born fifty years back, we would say that today's children lose their innocence at a faster pace. Why?

The reason for this is because we do not tell them who they really are. We focus on how they should look, dress, walk, and talk—to the extent that our children begin to believe that they are good if they get great grades or excel in sports or whatever our passion is.

Now, there is nothing incorrect about acquiring things; it is good to teach our children the competitiveness to acquire material things. However, we need to do it with an awareness of who we are and what we are acquiring. We need to dissociate from our ego and become aware of our real self.

We are not what we are acquiring…We are the soul, distinct from our physical body, distinct from our labels, distinct from our degrees and possessions!

Keeping the above things in mind, let us try to redefine ego.

Ego can be called an image that you create for yourself, an image that you are attached to, but it is not your true self.

Your true self is characterized by intentions, creativity, possibilities, and power.

The ego-image is characterized by masks, labels, and judgments.

> They are forever free who renounce all selfish desires and break away from the ego-cage of "I," "me," and "mine" to be united with the Lord.
>
> Attain to this, and pass from death to immortality. —*Bhagavad Gita*

There are three subdivisions of mind or mental principles, if we wish to call it that.

The first one is termed the **instinctive mind**—something that you share in common with the lower animals. In this phase, there is no consciousness. As it reaches the higher planes, this instinctive mind blends with what you call the **intellect** or **reason**.

In the lower phase, this instinctive mind helps in maintenance of animal life within your body; it supports the processes of digestion, assimilation, repair, replacement, and so on. This part of the mind is also a storehouse of your experiences from the past, and therefore, it becomes the center for envy, hatred, anger, jealousy, and so forth. All animal desires, such as thirst, hunger, and sexual desires, and passions such as envy, love, hatred, revenge, and jealousy are all seated in this part of the mind. This enables wearing specific masks, labels, or judgments. This leads to ego.

I do not condemn this instinctive mind. All the things seated there were necessary in the past, and some of them are still necessary in the present. This is your evolutionary mind. What needs to be understood here is that this part of the mind belongs to you; however, it is *not* "you."

Next comes your **intellect**. Intellect is the part of the mind that enables you to reason, think, or analyze. Once again, you are *using* the intellect; you are *not* the intellect! Therefore, this simply becomes a tool of your ego; it is not your real self, although you may sometimes imagine it to be so.

The third part of the mental principles is the **spiritual mind.** This part of the mind is the source of what you term "inspiration," "genius," or "spirituality." It is this part of the mind that enables the smooth flow of all consciousness.

In Eastern words, the intellect tries to move into the higher planes of spirituality, *aum* and *omkar*—toward eternal happiness and toward the Absolute. But the ego tries to move the intellect away from this plane into the realm of ahamkar—toward momentary pleasures and away from the Absolute.

In Western words, the ego tries to move the intellect away from "amen," the expression of surrender. The result is that you move from "amen" to "aiming"—attached mind-set—and once that process begins, you develop anger, fear, and pride…and the cycle goes on…

Here is a beautiful poem by Rabindranath Tagore that describes ego as "my own little self"':

> I came out alone on my way to my tryst.
>
> But who is this that follows me in the silent dark?
>
> I move aside to avoid his presence but I escape him not.
>
> He makes the dust rise from the earth with his swagger;
>
> He adds his loud voice to every word that I utter.
>
> He is my own little self, my lord, he knows no shame;
>
> But I am ashamed to come to thy door in his company.

Today, most people are utilizing the lower part of their brain; this is their instinctive mind.

Your goal must be to move from this lower plane toward intellect and then the spiritual mind. The human mind has a range of possibilities; all that is required is a shift from ego toward an awareness of who you really are; you are the soul residing in the spirit!

> Through delusion you are perceiving yourself as a bundle of flesh and bones, which at best is a nest of troubles. Meditate unceasingly, that you quickly behold yourself as the Infinite Essence, free from every form of misery. Cease being a prisoner of the body; using the secret key of Kriya, learn to escape into Spirit. —Lahiri Mahasaya

The Principle of Personal Energy Management

Imagine for a moment that you are a one-dimensional person who lives in a one-dimensional world. So, for this particular moment, you are like a dot on a piece of paper. This dot can only move in a straight line.

If we take one straight line and a dot on the center, the dot can either move toward the right or the left. It cannot move up or down.

And now, somebody grants you the power to live in a two-dimensional world. Wow! You are excited at your newfound ability to move up and down. You can even move in circles. So, you move out of the straight line and begin to move on the flat piece of paper—up and down, in circles, and right and left…

And one day you get bored with moving on this piece of paper and decide to take a small risk; you decide to jump.

And that's a revelation—you *can* jump.

You discover your newfound ability and now dance in a straight line, in circles, up and down on the piece of paper and occasionally you jump. The fact that now your existence is not limited to a flat piece of paper and you can achieve a fuller life makes you happy and joyful.

The realization that the possibilities are unlimited if you only try to break the barriers is amazing.

You love it, don't you?

You want to spread this joy all across the world, and in the process, you become an energy magnet.

You talk to other one-dimensional and two-dimensional dots and explain the exciting world of possibilities that awaits them. Some dots get your viewpoint and join you in your dance. They fall and get up again, excited at the possibilities life has to offer; they also begin to love the experience. Some are skeptical and wait for their friends to try it first.

Let us move into reality now. How do you perceive yourself today?

Humans have been taught the reality of three dimensions and therefore understand height, width, and depth. Almost everybody can move side to side, back and forth, in and out, and back and forth.

The question that I want to ask is if this is all that you are capable of.

Personally, I would term this as a limited perception of reality.

Because in reality, you are not a three-dimensional being.

You are much greater than that.

You are multidimensional; you are infinite!

That's the power that you possess.

Albert Einstein rightly said, "A new kind of thinking is essential if mankind is to survive and move toward higher levels."

This implies that you would need to alter your thinking process if you really want to alter your life.

Do you want to change your life for good?

Do you want to be happier?

If you answered in the affirmative, then you need to develop an understanding of who you are, the unlimited potential that you possess, the manner in which you interact with your fellow human beings, and the techniques that you deploy to elevate your natural abilities.

You possess the ability to utilize the power of thought and energy so that it impacts physical objects, helps you manifest your desires, and heals you spiritually. Utilization of this power brings in holistic happiness.

Your energy system is intelligent and alive. It understands exactly what is required for perfect health, harmony, and happiness. In case this system is slowed down, blocked, or damaged, messages are sent to the conscious level that something has gone wrong and needs to be fixed. Now you need to address these blockages, damages, and imbalances.

Currently, you are trained to look at your physical body and address its needs. In the process, you fail to observe your energy systems and therefore do not provide yourself the things that you need in order to achieve health, happiness, and harmony.

Your energy system is conscious energy that is *connected with the higher energy of the universe*. It is the *linkage between your physical world and the spiritual world.*

> The yogi who knows that the entire splendor of the universe is his, who rises to the consciousness of unity with the universe, retains his Divinity even in the midst of various thoughts and fancies...This entire universe is a sport of Consciousness. One who is constantly aware of this is certainly a liberated being (jivanmukta). —Hindu Tantric Scriptures

Addressing your energy blocks enables you to address your deepest needs—which could be physical, emotional, or spiritual.

Let me try to explain this in a little more detail.

Each and every living being is infused with a universal energy that nourishes and connects life. This energy has traditionally been called by various names, such as *prana,* and *chi.* Human beings are surrounded by an invisible energy field that is comprised of this energy.

Each and every life process in your body, mind, and soul—the manner in which your mind functions and you express your emotions, your spiritual life, and the operating system of your physical body—is necessarily supported via this energy field.

The energy in this energy field is active, intelligent, and full of life. It is this conscious energy that appears as an indicator of your universal consciousness, which is also the source of this entire universe. This energy, just like everything else in the universe, originates from the field of pure consciousness, which is also the spiritual origin of life. Infinite love, unlimited consciousness, infinite health, power, wellness, and knowledge are all born from this field of pure consciousness.

Each one of us possesses this consciousness individually, and yet, each one of us is connected and ultimately one.

> Man is shut up at present in his surface individual consciousness and knows the world only through his outward mind and senses and by interpreting their contacts with the world. By Yoga there can open in him a consciousness which becomes one with that of the world; he becomes

directly aware of a universal Being, universal states, universal Force and Power, universal Mind, Life, Matter and lives in conscious relations with these things. He is then said to have cosmic consciousness. —Aurobindo Ghosh, a Hindu philosopher and poet

Your association to this greatest spiritual reality lies within you; it lies in your vital nature, which tells you that you are pure consciousness, with unlimited power and knowledge inside your body.

Your personal energy field is made up of the *aura* (which manifests itself in seven layers) and the *chakra* system (which comprises the seven major *chakras*). It acts as a seven-step connection or the bridge between life and the field of pure consciousness present in this world. This energy field brings to life the unlimited potential and the infinite power that are characteristics of our spiritual being. It indicates and regulates the manner in which the life force or *chi* or *prana* exists within your field of pure consciousness and manifests itself in your worldly life.

Before getting into deeper detail of your personal energy field, let me first introduce you to the three kinds of energies that impact your happiness:

- your personal energy—the energy necessary for your personal well-being
- your social energy—the energy of the people whom you interact with every day
- your spatial energy—the energy of the space that you live in

You have the capability to demonstrate great health at each level—mental, physical, emotional, and spiritual—only if your energy field stays healthy, clear, and free from all defects and blockages.

The intrinsic harmony and health of your mind, body, and soul, the awareness of your spiritual self and your highest potential, manifests in your life by virtue of an integral connection to this field of pure consciousness, which enables the flow of these traits.

Many times, however, certain energetic defects appear in this energy field. An impure, weak, impaired, blocked, or unbalanced flow of energy prevents your connection with the ultimate spiritual reality or your field of pure consciousness. This field of pure consciousness is actually your true self.

The cause of these energetic defects can sometimes be traced to a psychological or a physical trauma. Any traumatic experience or a damaging life incidence or an unhealthy relationship in your past (this also includes your past lives) may sometimes not get completely assimilated by your psyche. This may result in excitation of an energy field with energetic defects. These energetic defects may disable you from establishing a complete connection between your true self and the ultimate reality, leaving some severe biases, which may also mean some unpleasant changes in your personality.

These energetic defects also establish unhealthy energies within your *aura* and *chakras*. As a result of this, the strong and healthy energy that is originally present in your energy field becomes compromised. This results in three kinds of defects:

- severe trauma to personality, which may also include some suppressed memories
- basic energetic defects within your aura and chakra system, which may include negative emotions and thoughts
- attack by unhealthy and impure energy, which is sometimes self-generated and sometimes enforced by others

It can also be said that these three defects very often exist together and are closely interrelated.

They also prevent the complete and healthy expression of your self-potential and eliminate the natural environment of energetic health that is a basic requirement for emotional, mental, physical, and spiritual well-being.

Talking about eliminating energy blockages, let us briefly touch upon the energy of auras, chakras, and *vastu*.

So, **what is an aura**?

We shall discuss this in detail later in the book, but for now, just to give you an idea, let us consider it as an energy field that engulfs, penetrates, and extends out your physical body. This energy field is electromagnetic and is composed of a number of intelligent or live frequencies. Another thing to be remembered is that the aura not only surrounds the human body; it surrounds every animate and inanimate thing in the universe.

The aura around conscious or living beings may vary with time, and it may change very quickly. However, the aura around nonliving beings remains fixed and may be altered by your conscious intent.

It is worth a mention that your aura comprises a number of layers—layers of mental, emotional, physical, and spiritual elements.

Sounds interesting, doesn't it?

Later chapters will help you explore more about your auras and how you can identify and correct blockages in them.

CHAPTER 4
The Spiritual Noumena

✷ ✷ ✷

HUMANS HAVE ALWAYS BEEN LINKED to a greater purpose or power.

We all feel that we have a spirit. There are definite indications around us that tell us that a higher order or a higher power exists—the changing of seasons, the germination of a seed, the rising of the sun, and more importantly, the strength within ourselves. Within us, we feel that we are more than just a body and mind.

What is this higher power that exists within us? It is our spirit. It is magical; it is the source of our overall strength.

Almost all saints, yogis, gurus, and Reiki masters believe that the only element that allows some comfort to humans in their day-to-day struggles is spirituality; this one element links all great people and beautifully so.

HOW WOULD I DEFINE SPIRITUALITY?
Well, to me spirituality is

- A "ritual" of the spirit—a way of life that helps me understand who I am and what my spirit is. Where does this spirit come from, and what is its purpose?

- A way to understand my complete personality—not just as a mind or a body but as a spirit, soul, mind, and body. Being material or being spiritual are two polarities of the being's one personality. Both polarities need to be understood for holistic happiness to be achieved.
- A multidimensional quality that comprises a quest for answers to some of life's big questions; I would call this a spiritual quest.
- A global view that rises above all ego.
- A sense of compassion and caring for the people in society; I would call this the ethics of compassion and caring.
- A lifestyle that believes in service to humanity; I would term this as some kind of charitable involvement.

To understand this more, let us go step-by-step.

We have already understood the ego or *aham*. We understand how we sometimes get attached to an incorrect image of our own self and in the process forget who we really are.

Let me ask you a simple question: "Who are you?"

You would immediately respond with your name, your job title, the street address where you live, your profession…and so on.

This means that you believe that everything that is "yours" is "you." And as your list of credentials, titles, possessions, and labels (indirectly ego) grows longer, you move away from the real "you."

So, the greater the list of labels, the farther you move from your own real self.

You are a human being.

The word *human* implies your physical body.

The word *being* implies your real self. It implies who you really are. And that is what spirituality does. It helps you move closer to yourself; it ends your search for your own self by introducing you to who you really are.

"Cease being a prisoner of the body; using the secret key of Kriya, learn to escape into Spirit." —Lahiri Mahasaya

You are a soul. You are the spirit.

Your body is made up of matter—which in reality is physical energy that can be seen, felt, or touched.

The other part of yourself—your real self—is composed of energy that can only be felt.

This is similar to a bulb of light that glows and provides light when it is supplied by electrical energy.

Can you see this electrical energy?

No!

But you can experience it through the lightening of the bulb.

Similarly, you—your real self, the spirit or the soul—cannot be seen; it can only be felt.

And just like the bulb is useless without the electrical energy, your physical body is useless without the soul or the spirit component.

A Peek into Your Heart
Your heart is beautiful.

As stated by Gautama Buddha, "The way is not in the sky. The way is in the heart."

And here is what the great Mahatma Gandhi had to say about the human heart: "In prayer, it is better to have a heart without words than words without a heart."

The *Chandogya Upanishad* defines your heart as, "There is a light that shines beyond all things on Earth, beyond us all, beyond the very highest heavens. This is the light that shines in our heart."

All these quotes strengthen our belief that the heart is the center of calmness or peace.

The Buddha mentioned, "Calmness is within you; do not look for it outside of you."

Now, you do not have to be Buddha to understand that opening your heart and using it properly can lead to deep peace and calmness; the ability to enjoy things better, pleasure, contentment, and wealth are only bonuses that you get along the way.

When I mention the term "heart" here, I am not talking about your physical heart. I am talking about your spiritual or nonphysical heart, which is located in the center of your chest. This heart is located in the heart chakra.

Now, this inner heart listens to the calling of your spirit and directs you toward the Absolute. This heart is pure.

Everyone possesses this heart. Even criminals possess it. The only problem is that this inner heart is closed in most individuals. **The power to open this heart is granted through the practice of raja-yoga, and once you possess that power, you get the ability to be directed toward the Absolute—your true source.**

Is there a connection between your heart and the Absolute?

Sure there is!

This connection is the connection of love. This divine connection defines how close you are to the Absolute.

> You could not in your travels find the source or destination of the soul, so deeply hidden is the Logos.
>
> [But] I searched for It [and found It] within myself.
>
> That hidden Unity is beyond what is visible.
>
> All men have this capacity of knowing themselves, [for] the soul has the Logos within it, which can be known when the soul is evolved.
>
> What is within us remains the same eternally;
>
> It is the same in life and death, waking and sleeping, youth and old age; for, It has become this world, and the world must return to It. —Heraclitus, pre-Socratic Greek philosopher

Talking from a spiritual point of view, human beings possess three levels of consciousness:

- physical and mental consciousness

- soul consciousness, and
- spirit consciousness

Let us try to explore this a little more.

To know God is the most important way to heal all disease—physical, mental, spiritual. As darkness cannot remain where light is, so also the darkness of disease is driven away by the light of God's perfect presence when it enters the body. — Paramahansa Yogananda

God is our Creator. Everything in the universe has its roots in God. If we review our most fundamental statement of faith, we would say that God is spirit. God does not possess a gender, creed, form, or color.

I refer to God as the Absolute. The reason I do is because if I asked you to think about God, you would probably think about a particular form, image, or picture.

When we talk about the Absolute or the *Brahm*, we do not look at the form or an image. And that is essentially what God is—without an image, gender, form, color, or creed. Sometimes I also refer to the Absolute as the Divine. For the ease of understanding, you can understand being divine as the innate nature of the Absolute. While the Absolute doesn't have a form, it does have a nature. Of course, the complete nature of the Absolute is infinite in expanse, unfathomable, and even unpredictable. Therefore, I use the word "divine" as a referential idea that points to the Absolute but without creating an image of a specific form in your mind.

Now, let us talk about you. Your spirit is the part of you that is directly created by the Absolute. It defines who you are and what you are in totality. It does not possess a color, form, character, or personality.

This spirit is one with all and understands the concept of oneness. It is one with the Absolute or the *Brahm*, but it is not the *Brahm*.

It has its roots in the *Brahm* and is perfect in every way.

> Aum
> Purnamadah Purnamidam
> Purnat Purnamudachyate
> Purnasya Purnamadaya
> Purnameva Vashishyate
> Om shanti, shanti, shanti.

This short verse from the Upanishads explains the nature of reality and the path to self-realization. The many translations available to understand this are:

> Om.
> That is infinite, this is infinite;
> From That infinite this infinite comes.
> From That infinite, if this infinite removed or added;
> Infinite remains infinite.
> Om. Peace! Peace! Peace!

> Om.
> That is full; this is full.
> This fullness has been projected from that fullness.
> When this fullness merges in that fullness,
> all that remains is fullness.
> Om. Peace! Peace! Peace!

> Om.
> Completeness is that, completeness is this,
> from completeness, completeness comes forth.
> Completeness from completeness taken away,

completeness to completeness added,
completeness alone remains.
Om. Peace! Peace! Peace!

Om.
Brahman is limitless, infinite number
of universes come out
and go into the infinite Brahman,
Brahman remains unchanged.
Om. Peace! Peace! Peace!

WHAT ABOUT THE SOUL?
Your soul is that aspect of your spirit that possesses human character and connects with human experiences.

And since your spirit is perfect, your soul becomes an expression of that perfection.

The soul guides you through the power of intuition and its connection with the spirit. It is often called your "higher self" and responds only to goodness.

The soul possesses conscience and, by the faculty of intuition, knows the difference between right and wrong, good and evil. It continuously evolves—through karma and through choice—and is always guided by the spirit, which, in turn, is always guided by the Absolute.

The soul can therefore be referred to as the "prodigal son" who seeks to return to the father.

In this scenario, the father is spirit, an eternal expression of the Absolute.

"Your purpose is not to save your soul, but to become more enlightened to the power and beauty of who you are, and to the divine creation of which we all are a part." —Trudy Vesotsky, founder and CEO at Behavioral Psychology Experts

The soul needs to incarnate onto the earth plane, and this is accomplished through the creation of a physical body—the ego or the personality.

This is your lower self—the self to which you identify if you have not developed a spiritual understanding.

To sum it up, you possess a spirit, which is always guided by the Divine or the Absolute.

You also possess a soul, which is guided by the spirit.

And then you possess an ego or a personality, which uses the power of your soul to exist but doesn't always obey the soul's guidance.

The soul is pure. But your personality may lead you to do evil; it may lead you to think negatively…How is this possible? Is this not a contradiction?

Well, this is because your personality can choose to accept or reject the guidance provided by your soul.

"Never think there is anything impossible for the soul. It is the greatest heresy to think so. If there is sin, this is the only sin; to say that you are weak, or others are weak." —Swami Vivekananda

This is a beautiful trinity of spirit-soul-personality—all three elements linking together to one Creator, who provides guidance, love, healing, and light.

Swami Parmahansa Yogananda explained this through the concept of the astral body and the physical body.

Your physical body is made up of sixteen chemical elements (sodium, potassium, chlorine, and so on, which are composed of protons, neutrons, and electrons). Two other bodies are hidden within this physical body; these are your astral body and your spiritual body. The astral body is further composed of nineteen elements (which are said to be composed of "lifetrons"). The spiritual body is composed of thirty-five elements. These are termed the "thoughtrons."

Your astral body is made up of nineteen elements, which are mental, emotional, and "lifetronic." Your physical form is built and maintained via these nineteen elements. These mental, emotional, and "lifetronic" abilities function from your center of life and consciousness, which is located in your astral brain and your chakras.

The nineteen elements are:

- Four functions of the mind—the *mana* or the *manas* (sense mind), *chitta* (feeling), *ahankara* (ego), and *buddhi* (intelligence)
- Five *pranas* (or life force)
- Ten *indriyas* (or your power of perception)
    - Five *jnanendriyas* (or the subtle power behind the physical senses of smell, hearing, touch, taste, and sight)
    - Five *karmendriyas* (or the power behind your ability to talk, walk, excrete, procreate, and exercise)

Your causal or the spiritual body is made up of thirty-five thoughts or thirty-five elements (the nineteen elements needed to create your astral body and the sixteen elements needed to create the material elements in your physical body).

To sum this up, just as astral energy is the cause of every physical energy, similarly, thoughtrons or causal elements are the cause of every astral mental element.

Then **what is spiritual evolution**?

According to Reiki raja-yoga, it is simply a process where you elevate your personality or ego and bring it to the level of the soul. You then elevate your soul and bring it to the level of spirit. And finally, you unravel your spirit and become one with the Absolute—you become enlightened! Understanding your true self through self-awakening and self-realization can help you in this process.

All right, **so what is death then**?

Death, as harsh as it may seem, is not a bad thing after all. It is that portal through which things material are separated from the spirit divine. What belongs to the Divine returns back to him, and what belongs to this *maya*-infested world is left here as ashes.

> The Self, having in dreams enjoyed the pleasures of sense, gone hither and thither, experienced good and evil, hastens back to the state of waking from which he started.
>
> As a man passes from dream to wakefulness, so does he pass from this life to the next.
>
> When a man is about to die, the subtle body, mounted by the intelligent self, groans—as a heavily laden cart groans under its burden.
>
> When his body becomes thin through old age or disease, the dying man separates himself from his limbs, even as a mango

or a fig or a banyan fruit separates itself from its stalk, and by the same way that he came he hastens to his new abode, and there assumes another body, in which to begin a new life.

When his body grows weak and he becomes apparently unconscious, the dying man gathers his senses about him and, completely withdrawing their powers, descends into his heart. No more does he see form or color without.

He neither sees, nor smells, nor tastes. He does not speak, he does not hear. He does not think, he does not know. For all the organs, detaching themselves from his physical body, unite with his subtle body. Then the point of his heart, where the nerves join, is lighted by the light of the Self, and by that light he departs either through the eye, or through the gate of the skull, or through some other aperture of the body. When he thus departs, life departs; and when life departs, all the functions of the vital principle depart. The Self remains conscious, and, conscious, the dying man goes to his abode. The deeds of this life, and the impressions they leave behind, follow him.

As a caterpillar, having reached the end of a blade of grass, takes hold of another blade and draws itself to it, so the Self, having left behind it [a body] unconscious, takes hold of another body and draws himself to it.

As a goldsmith, taking an old gold ornament, molds it into another, newer and more beautiful, so the Self, having given up the body and left it unconscious, takes on a new and better form, either that of the Fathers, or that of the Celestial Singers, or that of the gods, or that of other beings, heavenly or earthly." —The Upanishads

Death is simply the return of the personality back into the soul. In the process, the soul is reminded of all that it learned and experienced on the earth plane—this could be positive or negative.

The soul is guided by the spirit and has the power to decide how it will utilize the lessons that it has acquired from the personality. It has the power to make amendments through the great law of karma; these amendments can be made for the injustices or the harm that it may have caused to others or itself.

This is accomplished through successive incarnations—each with its own physical body or personality—to the point where the physical body becomes a perfect manifestation of the soul's purity and goodness. At this point, the soul no longer seeks incarnation; it just moves along in its evolution back to the spirit and reaches *nirvana*.

It takes one million years for the soul to perfect this process; however, this journey can be shortened by Reiki raja-yoga techniques. In fact, one of the techniques taught in this path of Reiki raja-yoga evolves the practitioner by one year in a single pranayama breath.

Most Eastern religions believe that the soul goes through many lives. It is believed that when a person dies, his or her soul enters a new body prior to that body's birth. This process continues till the time the soul reaches a state of *nirvana* and reunites with spirit and then the Absolute.

> na jayate mriyate va kadacin
> nayam bhutva bhavita va na bhuyah
> ajo nityah sasvato 'yam purano
> na hanyate hanyamane sarire. —*Bhagavad Gita*, chapter 2, verse 20

Sri Krishna says: The soul is never born nor dies at any time. Soul has not come into being, does not come into being, and will not come into being. Soul is unborn, eternal, ever-existing and primeval. Soul is not slain when the body is slain.

> vasamsi jirnani yatha vihaya
> navani grhnati naro 'parani
> tatha sarirani vihaya jirnany
> anyani samyati navani dehi. —*Bhagavad Gita,* chapter 2, verse 22

Sri Krishna has also said: As a human being puts on new garments, giving up old ones, the soul similarly accepts new material bodies, giving up the old and useless ones.

On reuniting with the Absolute, the soul may lose its identity, but it will not cease to exist. Consider a drop of water being poured into an ocean. This drop becomes a part of the ocean but does not cease to exist; it just becomes one with the ocean.

In summary, it can be said that:

- The earth plane or your physical body is the sum total of all that is. It was created at the time of conception and ceases to exist at the time of your death.
- As the real you or the soul leaves the physical body, it moves into another body to live...Therefore, life before and after death was always present and will always be present.
- The real you (or the soul) is eternal; you were created at a point in time that can be called timeless, and you shall always exist. After physical death, you live in other territories of spirit and gradually evolve in your consciousness. This leads to oneness with the Almighty.

- The only reason that you are provided the opportunity to live in the earth plane more than once is so that you can develop an understanding of this plane and that too, to the extent that you no longer require physical incarnation.
- Your life shall still continue as you become one with spirit and *Brahm* or the Holy Absolute.

Does this make sense?

There are people who believe that reincarnation is a myth.

I would say that there are a number of factors to support how reincarnation makes sense.

The first one would be that the process of reincarnation follows the law of cycles. History repeats itself, trees follow a cyclic pattern, seasons come and go...similarly, the cycle of rebirth is one of the many cycles that you are involved in.

My second and most powerful argument would be that reincarnation beautifully demonstrates the power of the Holy Absolute's grace, along with the ability that he provides you to correct the things that need to be corrected. The process of reincarnation ensures that the real you (or the soul) returns to the earth plane to relive some of your experiences; you are provided with the opportunity to become what you are capable of becoming! Reincarnation is the greatest demonstration of the faith that the Holy Absolute has in us. It demonstrates the deepest love that *Brahm* has for you—look at the opportunities you have been provided with.

Reincarnation also provides an opportunity to master your physical self or ego. You are given an opportunity to rise above the temptations of your physical body and consciously work with the inspiration of your spirit and, in turn, the Holy Absolute himself. You are able to cope with earthly experiences and reach a point where you do not need these experiences; that is the time when you do not come back into the earthly form—you achieve *nirvana* and become one with *Brahm*. It is evolution at a universal level.

Reincarnation explains *Brahm's* love and the powers that he provides you. The biggest power that he has provided you is the power of choice. You have the choice to live by the divine law or against it. In this process you become the master of your own destiny. Reincarnation offers you the opportunity to transform—from bad to good to great to greatest!

In your lifetime, your spiritual body sometimes aspires for direct divine guidance.

To be guided directly by the Divine, one must develop complete faith, nonattachment, and impartiality toward self-interests. Development of these qualities takes time.

> Why do you go to the forest in search of God?
> He lives in all and is yet ever distinct;
> He abides with you, too,
> As a fragrance dwells in a flower,
> And reflection in a mirror;
> So does God dwell inside everything;
> Seek Him, therefore, in your heart." —Guru Granth Sahib Adi Granth

CHAPTER 5
Karma, Samskaras, Sankalpas, and Avidya

✶ ✶ ✶

"The self-controlled person, moving among objects, with his senses free from attachment and malevolence and brought under his own control, attains tranquility."

— BHAGAVAD GITA

KARMA

The word *karma* means work, deed, or action. It could signify the action in itself or the result of a person's actions.

The most widely acknowledged and known definition of karma is "what goes around, comes around." Some people refer to it as "As you sow, so shall you reap."

Let us understand this a little more deeply.

Karma is neither a reward nor a punishment system.

When you look at the world around you, the first and the most obvious thing that you observe is the inequality in the world—some people are rich, some are poor, some are healthy, some are ill, some achieve all that they desire, and some struggle too hard to deserve what they desire. Is this merely an accident?

Absolutely not.

We cannot attribute this inequality to pure accident or blind chance. There has to be something else—something that links the entire thing.

Some people tend to believe that the main causes of this inequality are environment and heredity. This is true, but the connection with karma cannot be ruled out. Whatever you are, whatever you achieve, is a result of your past actions or your present doings. In fact, it is karma that governs our environment and heredity as well.

You are responsible for creating your own heaven or hell. You are the architect of your happiness or misery—to the extent that you decide your fate.

"You alone are responsible for yourself. No one else may answer for your deeds when the final reckoning comes. Your work in the world—in the sphere where your Karma, your own past activity, has placed you—can be performed only by one person: yourself." —Paramahansa Yogananda

Mystified by the seemingly incomprehensible, evident disparity that existed among humanity, a young truth-seeker approached the Buddha and asked him about this problem:

> "What is the cause, what is the reason, O Lord," questioned he, "that we find amongst mankind the short-lived and long-lived, the healthy and the diseased, the ugly and beautiful, those lacking influence and the powerful, the poor and the rich, the low-born and the high-born, and the ignorant and the wise?"

Here is the Buddha's reply:

> "All living beings have actions (Karma) as their own, their inheritance, their congenital cause, their kinsman, their refuge. It is Karma that differentiates beings into low and high states." — *Culla Kamma Vibhanga Sutta*

Swami Paramahansa Yogananda said:

> The habits you cultivated in past lives have substantially created your physical, mental, and emotional makeup in this life. You have forgotten those habits, but they have not forgotten you. Out of the crowded centuries of your experiences, your Karma follows you. And whenever you are reborn, that Karma, consisting of all your past thoughts and actions and habits, creates the kind of physical form you will have—not only your appearance, but your personality traits. It is these individually created past-life patterns that make one person different from another, and account for the great variety of human faces and characteristics. The very fact that you are a woman or a man was determined by your self-chosen tendencies in previous lives.

This can be further explained through the law of cause and effect.

Each one of us is born with specific hereditary characteristics. The interesting part is that at the same time, each one of us is also blessed with certain innate abilities that science cannot adequately explain.

We are indebted to our parents for the gross ovum and sperm that create the nucleus of our so-called being. We can also say that this ovum and sperm remain dormant within each parent until this potential germinal compound is invigorated by the karmic energy needed for the production of the fetus.

Hence, if I were to mention one indispensable conceptive cause of this being, I would say "Karma."

Another interesting fact that needs to be understood here is that accrued karmic tendencies, inherited during the course of previous lives, generally play a far greater role than the genes and the hereditary parental cells in the development of both mental and physical characteristics.

To explain this through an example, if we were to analyze the life of the Buddha, we could very easily say that like every other person, he inherited the reproductive cells and genes from his parents. However, if we compare him to his long line of royal ancestors, we know that physically, morally, and intellectually there was none like him.

In his own words, he mentioned that he belonged to the Aryan Buddhas and not to the royal lineage. It would not be incorrect to call him a creation of his own karma.

This unique example makes it obvious that karmic tendencies not only impact our physical organism, but also invalidate the potentiality of parental genes and cells.

"We are the heirs of our own actions." —The Buddha

Some secrets definitely echo through time. The world as you see it today is simply a reflection of your past. The manner in which you act today will create your future. Every single thing that you are experiencing at this moment is what karma wants you to experience. Every thought, feeling, and action has been created especially for you just so that you can learn from your past. The compact disc (CD) of your life has already been recorded based on your past karma; it is just playing through the player of life.

"Before you act, you have freedom, but after you act, the effect of that action will follow you whether you want it to or not. That is the law of Karma." —Paramahansa Yogananda

The universe makes every effort to complete your knowledge of the world. This ensures that you learn from your karma and also from the suffering of others. It empowers you to look at life from a number of different perspectives. A karmic experience can enable you to ponder upon and correct your mistakes.

Your life can also be described as a certain amount of energy controlled by a certain amount of information. Let us call this information "software." This software charges a certain amount of life energy in order to produce a certain kind of information technology; this information technology is *you*.

The kind of character that you become is dependent upon the type of information that has gone into you. It must be remembered that the past impressions of life go far beyond the moment you were born. However, at least from the moment you were born till today, the kind of parents you get, the family values that you acquire, and the education that you attain, along with your religious and social background and cultural realities, help in shaping your character.

The kind of information that goes inside a person enables him or her to acquire a particular type of character. Everybody is different—primarily because of the manner in which information is fed into his or her system. This is what we refer to as karma.

Traditionally, your karma is imprinted in your causal body, and this is what leads to life.

This information appears on many different levels. Let us first look at level one or the *sanchita karma*. The sanchita karma can be termed as the warehouse of karma, and it goes right back into the single-celled animals from where life is said to have evolved. It is important to understand that all information is right up there. You just need to close your eyes, become aware, and look into your own self; you will amazed at how you are able to understand the nature of the universe.

The reason that you understand this is not because you are looking at it through your head, but because all this information is present during the creation of your body. Your sanchita karma is a warehouse of information that goes back into creation. It is a result of your past actions that is responsible for future births. It is your primitive karma that is present in you when you are born.

Can you take this warehouse and practice retail business?

Well, you would need a shop for that, wouldn't you? This shop is referred to as *parabdha karma*.

Prarabdha karma can be explained as a certain or specific amount of information that has been allocated for this life. You must understand that life allots each person a specific amount of information, which is dependent on the vibrancy of your life and the information that you can take on. It is a result of your past deeds and present birth.

This also demonstrates that creation is immensely compassionate. It prevents you from dying by not giving you the whole lot of karma. A number of individuals seem to be tortured by simple memories from forty to fifty years of this lifetime. Just imagine what would happen if they were given a hundred times that memory. Obviously, they would not be able to survive it. Therefore, nature allocates prarabdha karma in just the right amount of memory that you can handle.

Prarabdha karma can also be *sthaanbaddh* or *samaybaddh karma*. *Sthanbaddh karma* manifests only at a certain place. As an example, a change in place may lead you to fall sick. *Samaybaddh karma* manifests itself at a certain time. Everything may be going well in your life, and suddenly, at the age of thirty, something bad happens…and then the next thing happens…and sometimes you don't even know what's wrong; you are just left to figure out how things have gone out of control since you reached thirty.

The science of Reiki raja-yoga gives you the power to work out your karma in such a way that you can achieve holistic happiness in your life and progress into self-realization. Through the self-healing techniques of Reiki, you can actually dissolve both your prarabdha karma and sanchita karma and avert any mishap that is about to manifest on the physical plane. Of course, the amount of karma you dissolve depends on the intensity of your Reiki raja-yoga daily practice.

A third kind of karma is *kriyamana karma*, which is a result of the actions that you perform in your present life.

What happens when you decide to take on the spiritual path?

In this scenario, you want to reach your ultimate destination, and that at lightning-fast speed.

In that process, you really don't want to take one hundred lifetimes. If you were to take a hundred lifetimes, you would be able to gather enough karma that could last you for another hundred lifetimes.

But you want to rush this up and move at lightning-fast speed...

Once the process of spiritual realization begins, when Reiki raja-yoga initiations are performed in a correct manner, it opens up dimensions that would not have opened otherwise.

And it provides you the power to decide the pace.

A number of seekers believe that embarking on a spiritual journey makes everything crystal clear for them. This depends on how you take it; if you want to move at a fast pace, things actually become blurred (at least initially). Imagine the beautiful countryside view and you driving at two hundred miles per hour. Would you be able to enjoy the scenic beauty in this scenario? Perhaps not. The speed that you decide to move with decides how much you enjoy or gain along the path.

You even have the power to alter your karma. You may not be able to stop it, but you can definitely change it. You can undo the wrongdoings of the past by doing good now.

You have already reaped what you sowed. It is now your choice to recreate your destiny. You are blessed with that free will.

Being aware of your actions, learning from them, and investing a substantial amount of time and effort on good things can enable you to change your karma.

The path of Reiki raja-yoga enables you to work out your karma through visions and dreams. This can prevent the karma from manifesting itself in your so-called real life.

The universe allows us to correct one form of energy using another form of energy. This is the law of energy exchange. It is also the law of karma.

This process was made possible by grace. Without it, bad energy would remain uncorrectable.

The process of energy exchange is free, but the mind sees only the giving side of it; therefore, it appears to you as not free.

Spiritually ignorant karma or actions create mental and auric blocks. And these become the root cause of unhappiness.

To sum up,

- Sanchita karma and prarabhdha karma are your destiny (or fate). They can also be collectively called your karmic will (in contrast to your free will).
- The alignment of your free will with your destiny determines your experiences in this life.
    - If your free will is aligned with your destiny completely, you experience life as easy and smooth.
    - If your free will is somewhat aligned with your destiny, then the experiences of life are a mixed bag.
    - If your free will is completely opposite to your destiny in this life, you will experience life as difficult and laden with obstacles.
- Through the meditation and healing techniques of Reiki raja-yoga, your past karma works out at a faster pace than it normally

would. Therefore, any opposing force exerted by your destiny karma on your free will is reduced. You then experience your life in line with what you desire your life to be.
- Another approach is that you completely surrender your free will, that is, have no desires, and let your past karma work out completely. This approach is practiced in the devotional paths of spirituality. Eventually, when all your past karma is worked out, you have no destiny. Your free will becomes your destiny. However, this may take hundreds and even thousands of years in its normal course.
- The philosophy of Reiki raja-yoga teaches that you should use a combination of self-effort and surrender to the Divine to work out your karma. This is the most practical and faster way to mend your destiny and achieve holistic happiness.

The deeper teachings of Reiki raja-yoga also reveal that while holistic happiness can be achieved by working out the hard karma and by generating good karma, to achieve self-realization you need to further penetrate into the deepest recesses of your personality. You need to do this to further understand and cure the conditioning of your ego, intellect, and mind at the deepest and the subtlest level. Many meditation and Yoga practices stop at karma. They fail to address the much more subtle and deeper conditioning that keeps you ignorant about your true self. This deeper conditioning is referenced as *samskaras* and *sankalpas*. I must warn you that even the advanced scriptures of Yoga have a variety of definitions of this deeper level of conditioning. I am describing this conditioning for the sake of completeness of this book. Their true nature can only be understood through experience under the proper guidance of a Reiki raja-yoga master.

SAMSKARAS
A number of people understand samskaras to be rituals or sacrifices.

In order to introduce you to samskaras, I shall first briefly explain the concepts of *vritti* and *chitta*.

Vritti emerges as a thought wave or a whirlpool that arises in your mind ocean. It is functional for some time and then sinks below the threshold of normal consciousness. It continues to sink from the conscious mind into the subconscious mind, which is often referred to as the *chitta*. Inside the chitta, it continues to remain in subliminal action and takes the form of a samskara.

We can therefore define samskaras as impressions; these could be cognitive, conative, or affective and adopt a latent or potential form just below the threshold of consciousness.

It is possible to recall past experiences from the storehouse of samskaras located in the subconscious mind. Every single detail about the past is preserved here. For example, if a person has an otherwise unexplainable fear of water, then through deep meditation it is possible for her to access her samskaras and recall any water-related accident that she might have had in a previous birth. This recollection can help dispel the fear of water by removing the samskara of the accident from her chitta.

Sometimes external stimuli can awaken related samskaras in the mind.

When you look at an apple and taste it for the first time, you become conditioned about the appearance and taste of the apple. This leads to the formation of a samskara in your subconscious mind. Next time when you look at another apple, the related samskara awakens and creates an expectation of its taste.

To connect the dots, vrittis (proclivities) create chitta (subconscious mind), and vice versa, chitta gives rise to vrittis. Over a period of time, these create samskaras (deep impressions) on the chitta.

Samskaras work like forces; they may support or inhibit one another. When you spot a person who needs your monetary help, your samskaras of sharing and caring attitude come into action, and you notice yourself helping this person.

A child is born as a storehouse of samskaras, which are engraved in the chitta that forms the seat of prarabdha. During his life, this child gains a number of other experiences or samskaras that get added to his store and manifest as the future sanchita karma.

The nature of your thoughts and desires is dependent on the nature of your samskaras. Great samskaras lead to great desires, and bad samskaras result in bad actions and thoughts.

Can you develop good samskaras?

Absolutely!

The practice of Reiki and raja-yoga acts as a facilitator in your journey to achieve great samskaras and good karma leading to self-realization.

"Tajjah Samskaro anya Samskara pratibandhi."

"The *Samsakaras* of true knowledge experienced through *Samadhi* (the highest state of meditation) prevents new *Samskaras* from forming." —Patanjali's Yoga Sutra I.50

Sankalpas

A sankalpa is commonly understood as a thought or an idea that may arise from within. In contrast to a samskara, a sankalpa may not need any external stimulus.

Sankalpa has other meanings as well. One of the esoteric meanings is that a sankalpa is a delusional idea or concept that the Absolute consciousness brings upon itself. It is this idea that separates the Absolute from the spirit, the spirit from the soul, and the soul from the personality. So, from an Absolute standpoint, spirit, soul, ego, intellect, mind, and everything else are just concepts!

Only the Absolute truly is. The rest are just concepts created by the Absolute.

To advanced yogis, I define sankalpas as the fundamental concepts that define your very being. These concepts are much deeper than the samskaras. These are concepts assumed by the self to define its own self. You have assumed a definition that you are a human, and that you are male or female, black or white. Within an overarching abstract concept are embedded other loosely defined concepts, and within those are embedded more defined concepts and so on.

Sankalpas are limiting concepts of which your ego-personality (*aham*) is made. They are so deeply embedded within your being that they are the hardest to recognize and to dispel. These concepts persist even after you work out your past karma, annul the vrittis, and purify the chitta.

The sankalpas are the building blocks of the being. They are the building blocks used by *maya* or the Absolute's cosmic hypnosis to create this illusory universe. As mentioned earlier, maya is that which can be measured. In other words, maya is that which limits, and sankalpas are limiting concepts. But then, maya is also a concept. So maya is also a sankalpa!

The realization of the Absolute can be initiated through the mind through intelligent practice of rooting out of the sankalpas.

How can you destroy sankalpas?
Let me ask you a question here: What happens when you try to bury your own shadow in the ground? It obviously comes out.

Similarly, if you try to eradicate the sankalpas through vritti (the whirlpool of thoughts), they will tend to emerge again.

You have to go "beyond thought" to destroy the bondage of sankalpas.

You need to withdraw your mind from the manifested world under the careful guidance of a spiritual guru. Do not overthink about how things are happening in the universe. Keep logic by the wayside and develop a deeper understanding of your mind through meditation. Focus on the Holy Absolute because that is where there are no concepts.

Directing all your thoughts on the Absolute will lead to annihilation of sankalpas. This secret is revealed in the path of Reiki raja-yoga.

Eradication of sankalpas will lead to elimination of *avidya*, which is the root cause of all unhappiness.

Avidya
Avidya is spiritual ignorance.

In order to understand avidya, we will have to look at the three *gunas* or the three basic qualities in a human being's character.

Simply speaking, *guna* can be defined as your character or your basic qualities. In reality, the concept of gunas is much more than this simple definition. You can also call these gunas your impulses. These are contained in your mind and become the foundation for all existence.

There is no specific translation available for these three gunas in the English language; however, the best way to explain them is as below:

- *sattva* (purity or knowledge)
- *rajas* (passion or action)
- *tamas* (ignorance or inertia)

Avidya can be defined as that condition of the mind in which sattva is subordinated to rajas and tamas. This is often referred to as the malina sattva, since it is considered as impure due to the predominance of rajas and tamas.

Patanjali describes avidya in the following words: "Ignorance is perceiving the non-eternal, impure, evil, and what is not soul, to be eternal, pure, good, and the soul" (Yoga Sutra II:5).

The experiences of this world are a result of the force of avidya. It is this force of avidya that drowns you into the ocean of samskara. This negative power ensures that you forget your divine nature. Desire, pleasure, pain, karma, delusion, pride, attraction, repulsion, egoism, lust, jealousy, and anger are all effects of avidya.

You can look at avidya as the source of all misery, sin, or ignorance. It has no beginning but surely possesses an end.

Avidya terminates the moment you begin to understand yourself. It is often called the absence of knowledge or erroneous knowledge.

It is simply not possible to define the nature of avidya because it is not real; it vanishes the moment you begin to understand yourself. It is not even unreal because you do experience it. You cannot call it a nonentity since it can be destroyed by self-knowledge. It is this force of avidya that allows you to mistake the pure immortal self as the impure mortal body, which then makes statements such as, "I am lean, beautiful, handsome, a homemaker, an engineer, a doctor," and so on.

Through the Reiki raja-yoga meditations, once you begin to understand yourself, you begin to understand the how and why of avidya. This leads to the removal of those karmic blocks and samskaras that not only block your holistic happiness, but also stunt your self-realization.

This chapter covered the fundamental concepts in the philosophy of Reiki raja-yoga. Depending upon what holistic happiness means to you, you will need to work out your karma and, to a great extent, the samskaras that are holding you back. For self-realization to happen, a much deeper transformation of all your karma, samskaras, and sankalpas, leading up to the removal of the veil of avidya, needs to happen under the direction of a spiritual master. The knowledge provided in this chapter, just by the process of reading and absorbing, will start progressing you toward holistic happiness.

CHAPTER 6
The Aura and the Chakras

✷ ✷ ✷

DIVINE HEART CONTAINS AN INFINITE cloud of integral self-awareness.

This cloud holds an invisible ocean of pure love and supreme intelligence.

When it rains, the holy water or aum, germinates the seeds of karma.

The effect is a body with an aura contained within the mind, epicentered in the soul.

Aura is the reservoir created from this rain.

Mind, like a tap, controls how much water enters the aura.

Aura blocks are leaks that drain the water.

The quality of our life directly depends on the level of water in the reservoir of our aura.

We are reservoirs of love and intelligence—large, small, and sometimes dry.

We all have access to the ocean of love and intelligence; it is free and surrounds us all the time.

Free your ego, make your mind free of limited concepts, and remove the leaks in your aura reservoir.

The ocean will flow in automatically to fill the reservoir.

This is the karmic law.

Everything in this universe is simply a vibration. Every atom, part of an atom, electron, proton, and neutron is a vibration. This vibration creates a field of energy. This field of energy is called an *aura*. In fact, your consciousness and your thoughts have subtle vibrations too.

An aura is sometimes described as an electro-photonic vibration response of an object to some external excitation (such as an ambient light, for example). In a living being, it can also be called a bioenergy field that penetrates, engulfs, and spreads out beyond the physical body.

Aura is a Western term. According to the Eastern yogic scriptures, human beings have five *koshas* or sheaths in their body. These are:

1. *annamaya* kosha—physical sheath
2. *pranmaya* kosha—energy sheath
3. *manomaya* kosha—emotional sheath
4. *gyanmaya* kosha—mental/intellectual sheath
5. *anandmaya* kosha—causal sheath or the radiance of the soul

To relate the concept of the aura with Eastern teachings, koshas 2, 3, and 4 can be considered as the human aura. Sometimes in Western teachings, koshas 1 through 5 are all referred to as the aura to keep things simple.

From a yogic point of view, the aura is created by the energy generated by the chakras. The aura is the projection of energy from the chakras.

Western science understands the aura as electromagnetic and encompassing various kinds of live and intelligent vibrations. Through science we understand that electromagnetic radiation ranges from microwave and infrared (IR) to UV light. The levels of physical functioning of your body (DNA structure, metabolism, circulation, etc.) are impacted by the low-frequency microwave and infrared part of the spectrum (body heat), whereas the high-frequency or the UV part of the spectrum is connected to your conscious activity, such as creativity, sense of humor, intentions, thinking, and emotions.

An aura not only surrounds every living thing, including animals, plants, and humans; it also engulfs and penetrates each inanimate object, including the objects created by man. Celestial bodies such as the sun, moon, stars, earth, and all other planets in this universe also have an aura.

The human aura has layers of physical, emotional, mental, and spiritual elements. The aura around conscious or living beings has the tendency to vary with time, and may change very quickly at times. However, the aura around nonliving beings is generally fixed and can only be altered by your conscious intent.

WHAT ARE AURAS MADE UP OF?
The energy field projected by your chakras becomes your aura.

An aura is made up of astral lights and energies of the colors of the rainbow at any given time. The aura changes its colors depending upon the emotions that you are experiencing. I am calling these colors astral because they can't be seen with the physical eyes by an average person. These colors are seen, or in most cases felt, when the observer's third-eye chakra (we will read more about the third-eye chakra later) becomes active such that it can perceive these colors. Such an activation of the third-eye chakra can also empower the physical eyes such that the physical eyes can see these astral colors in a similar way as they see physical colors. Such people are said to have the psychic ability to see the auras; they are also called clairvoyant because they can look at your aura and, based on the patterns of the aura, can describe what is happening and may happen in the future in your life and your physical body. The colors and patterns of the aura change constantly. This change in colors and patterns demonstrates endless alterations in your thoughts and emotions.

The aura is enhanced through loving and happy thoughts and diminished through angry and sad thoughts.

Does the aura have a definite size?

Your aura has the capability to adjust its size depending on the density of the population where you live. Egoistic thoughts and emotions, fear, illness, and so on weaken your connection with the universe and can shrink your aura or make it dull.

Spiritual masters have auras that can extend from hundreds of feet to miles in some cases. As the consciousness of a spiritual master evolves and expands, there comes a time when the aura of the master becomes limitless because it merges with the aura of the universe.

The important thing to understand about an aura is that it contains important information about you. This information can give a spiritual healer insight into your true state of mind and, also, into the events that are about to happen in your life. It is also important that when you approach a spiritual healer to get your aura read, you be open to the spiritual healer. Not being open to the spiritual healer can cause limited information to be visible to the healer, which in turn will affect his or her analysis of your state and any proposed remedies. I, personally in my practice, respect the privacy of my initiates and do not forcefully try to tune into their aura without their will.

The aura also becomes your spiritual signature. You possess a spiritually advanced personality if your aura appears to be clean and bright. An individual with a dark or gray aura demonstrates unclear intentions. However, most people are not even aware of their aura.

AND WHAT DO AURAS EXACTLY CONSIST OF?
Different spiritual traditions describe the constituents of the aura differently. The practice of Reiki raja-yoga respects all the reasonable definitions of what the aura consists of. Reiki raja-yoga lays emphasis on you doing your own practice and coming to your own *realization* of your aura.

All the concepts that describe the aura are basically trying to grade and classify a continuum of energy that is beyond your physical body. There is also a continuum of different states of your mind that corresponds to this energy continuum. **This energy and mental continuum bridges your physicality with your spirituality**. Eastern seers divide this continuum into the five sheaths or koshas mentioned earlier. Western scholars divide the same continuum into seven sheaths. You can understand the aura in terms of as many sheaths as needed to aid your understanding of your own self.

To help your rational and inquisitive mind understand, let me further describe the aura from a Western viewpoint as being made up of seven sheaths. These sheaths are called auric bodies in Western texts. Each one of these intelligent bodies that exist around the physical body possesses its own unique vibration. All these bodies are interconnected and impact one another and the person's emotions, feelings, behavior, thinking, and health. Hence, any imbalance in one of these bodies results in an imbalance in the others.

Let us take a look at these auric bodies along with your needs at each level of the auric field:

- The physical *auric* body—This impacts your physical sensations (including simple physical comfort, health, and pleasure).
- The etheric auric body—This impacts your emotions with respect to your own self (including self-acceptance and self-love).
- The vital *auric* body—This impacts your rational mind (including your ability to understand the situation in a clear and rational manner).
- The astral (emotional) body—This impacts relations with others (including loving interaction with family and friends).
- The lower mental *auric* body—This impacts the divine will within you (including the ability to align with the divine will, to follow the truth, and to make commitment to speak).
- The higher mental *auric* body—This impacts divine love and spiritual ecstasy.
- The spiritual (intuitive) body—This impacts the divine mind and the serenity within (including the connection with the Divine and the understanding of the greater universal pattern).

The meaning of colors

Your aura is a reflection of the true state of your mind. The state of your mind in due course of time translates into the experiences that you have in life; therefore, the aura is, in fact, your destiny that is about to happen.

Spiritual healing of the aura through Reiki raja-yoga techniques can change your destiny.

The color and intensity of the aura, especially above and surrounding your head, have a definite meaning.

As a general rule, a spiritually advanced person will have a colorful and bright aura. Also, uniform energy distribution in the aura implies that the person is balanced and healthy.

Most people have one or two predominant colors in their aura. These colors are often their favorite colors.

In addition to these colors, auras also demonstrate the presence of flashes, flames, or clouds. These reflect desires, thoughts, feelings, and energy blocks.

Sometimes dark clouds are seen in the aura. These represent energy blocks or the presence of elementals. Elementals are parasitic negative beings that don't have a physical body. The elementals latch on to the aura of the host and draw energy from the host. This depletes the energy of the host, who feels tired for no reason and experiences hardships or blocks in life despite making efforts.

These colors are not physical colors but are sensed intuitively by a spiritual master or healer who uses his or her third eye to sense the color and the spiritual or material element in the color.

Purple color: The presence of purple color in an aura is indicative of spiritual thoughts. Darker shades of purple represent an individual who is spiritual but is also rational in his or her understanding of spirituality. Shades of whitish purple indicate the development of faith in the person; such a person spontaneously experiences the Absolute through faith rather than through complicated logic. Changes in the shades of purple from dark to bright to white represent a journey from rationality to faith. For example, a Vedic pundit who understands God through the theoretical explanation of the *Vedas* will have dark purple color in the aura, whereas a meditating yogi who has not read the *Vedas* but experiences God through meditation and, hence, has developed faith will show whitish purple and brilliant white colors in his or her aura.

Indigo color: Represents wisdom and intuition.

Blue color: Represents expansion in understanding. It is the color of sky and space. A mature understanding of the world. Patience. Peace. Survivor.

Green color: Signifies joy and healing.

The presence of green color is indicative of natural healing ability. It signifies a restful and a joyful energy. Most natural healers have a green strong point in their aura. The stronger the green aura, the better the healer. The company of a person with a strong and green aura can be an extremely restful and joyful experience.

However, a dirty green color can signify a greedy or overattached personality.

Yellow/Golden color: Represents material achievement and knowledge.

The presence of yellow/golden color in the aura is indicative of the power of achievement and ability to acquire knowledge. People who glow golden are able to achieve their goals and appear full with confidence and are able to manifest abundance in their lives. A golden halo around the head is indicative of a high level of life-force energy. This golden halo appears as a consequence of a fully active back third-eye chakra that has been meditated upon for a number of years. As a result of meditation, golden-colored life-force or *pranic* energy accumulates around this chakra on the back of the head.

Orange color: This represents understanding of the purpose of life. It also represents creativity and passion in general and also the passion to achieve the purpose of life. Renunciant monks in India wear orange- or saffron-colored robes to balance the passionate aspect of their human nature and to direct their creativity and passion toward spiritual purposes.

Red color: The color red signifies materialistic thoughts and thoughts about the physical body. A predominantly red aura is indicative of a materialistic person.

It also represents the will to live. Strong red color indicates a person grounded in the reality that can be validated by the physical eyes; such a person understands, responds to, and believes only that which can be physically seen.

Pink color (= purple + red): This is indicative of love (in a spiritual sense). In order to achieve a clean pink, you would need to mix the purple (the highest frequency we perceive) with red (the lowest frequency). A pink aura is indicative of a person who has achieved a perfect balance between spirituality and materialism. The most advanced people not only possess a golden halo around the head but also demonstrate a large pink aura extending farther away. The pink color indicates the presence of Reiki in a person's aura. After initiation into Reiki raja-yoga, the pink color in the aura is enhanced multiple times.

Is it possible to enhance your aura or the energy field?
As you remember that your aura also influences the things and people you come in contact with along with impacting your own personality, you understand the need to develop a strong aura.

In order to enhance your aura, you may:

- directly flood your aura with the best vibrations by means of holding in your mind clear, distinct pictures of desirable feelings and objects.
- It also helps to visualize a flood of brilliant white light flooding the aura like a waterfall from the top of your head to the base of your feet, cleansing all the blocks and balancing the abnormalities in the aura.
- Use the added impact of colors, beads, and so on to the ideas that are deemed desirable and worthy of development. These beads or objects can be charged with energies of healing and protection.

Reiki and raja-yoga offer specific techniques that can enable you to strengthen your aura. Specific beads and energy instruments provided to you by your spiritual guru can help in creating energy of protection and healing your mind and body. These are generally preprogrammed to emanate healing energies.

In summary, I would say that eternal happiness is your highest achievement and all achievements are the result of your personal energy field or the aura, which is, in turn, directed through your mind.

Avidya or spiritual ignorance can lead to auric blocks, which can further lead to unhappiness. Reiki and raja-yoga help in healing these energy blocks so that you can progress toward eternal happiness.

Understanding the Chakras

Let me first ask you, "How well do you understand yourself?"

You do recognize yourself, correct? You look into the mirror and see a beautiful you gazing back at you.

Now, that's what we term a miracle of science.

Many times your friends and family members look at you and try to judge you. And sometimes, they just let you be you. They can look at you, feel you, and quite often even understand how you feel—simply because they are blessed with a wonderful pair of eyes and, of course, a great mind.

Should this be termed as nature's miracles? Sure; they are.

Now, let me introduce you to a part of you that nobody knows and understands.

That person in the mirror cannot look at this part of you. Your friends and family who understand you also do not know this part of you.

This chapter provides you the undisclosed key to unlock this secret code that you possess. Unlocking this secret code can lead you toward a greater level of self-awareness or realization.

I am talking about *chakras*—the seven vortices of energy spinning inside your body. These vortices of energy are placed along your spine, beginning from the bottom of your pelvis and moving up to the crown of your head.

And these chakras can reveal more information about you than anything or anybody else can.

When you gain an understanding about your chakras, you gain an understanding about your own self.

Harnessing the power of chakras can enable you to draw maximum benefits for yourself. Understanding the chakras helps you understand why you feel an imbalance when you feel an imbalance and how you can overcome that imbalance through the power of your spinning energy wheels.

Before you read further, take a deep breath, sit back, and relax—because as you read further, you will move into a higher stage of self-realization and personal evolution; slowly you will get to understand yourself and then connect with the Divine.

Imbalance in chakras can also lead to mental and physical ailments. Sure, there are several other factors that lead to formation of disease in the human body; however, it is worthwhile to understand that an imbalanced chakra enhances that likelihood.

Just break this word up: disease…dis-ease…lack of ease…lack of balance…chakra imbalance.

There is definitely a connection.

I have some more questions for you.

Would you want to sit in the driving seat of your own life? Would you want to have better control over your life and integrate your whole self into actually feeling "whole"? Are you courageous enough to explore the underlying meaning of your symptoms? Would you want to feel empowered enough so that you understood your body, mind, and spirit? And would you like to look at means that can enable you to harmonize your body, mind, and spirit?

The journey ahead is going to be immensely exciting. And don't worry about the pace; we will take it slowly—one step at a time.

So, *what are these chakras?*

Before we get there, let me ask you something. Have you noticed that there are some days when you are feeling on top of the world? These are usually the days when you are your chirpiest best, you want to talk to everybody, you feel like dancing around and having loads of fun. For no evident reason, you want to celebrate the day by donning your best outfit and spending time with your best pals. And then there are other days—these are the days when you are so low that, forget talking, you do not want to look at anyone. All you want to do is shut yourself in a room and just be alone—you do not even understand the reason why you are feeling so low.

Sometimes you are just thinking about somebody, and that person visits your house. You often dismiss this as a coincidence.

And sometimes, when you achieve some happiness, *you begin to believe that there may be some higher power that knows what you want and this higher power does everything right in order to get this thing for you.*

Here is an interesting fact: all these natural feelings are actually emitted like rays out of your own body. They are radiated by your chakras or energy centers.

The ancient Indian texts refer to chakras as the vortices of energy inside your body. What is important is an understanding that these chakras do not relate to your physical body. They are a part of your energy body and hence cannot be detected by any MRI or X-ray. They have the power to directly influence your mental, physical, emotional, and spiritual condition.

The chitta or your subconscious mind is directly connected to your astral body, which contains the first five chakras. This implies that your mind is connected to these chakras and this influences your ability to react to a particular situation. The decision-making part of your brain receives messages from the chakras, and this helps you decide the manner in which you should be reacting to a particular situation.

It sometimes seems like a contradiction. How is it possible for something to exist when you cannot see it?

The fact is that even though you cannot see your chakras, you can still feel them.

Let us look at a few examples here:

- Have you ever experienced butterflies in your stomach as you think about your perfect date or the person of your dreams? This is your second chakra in action.
- Have you ever visited a place where the toilets are not as clean as you would like them to be? Do you notice how you begin to instantaneously feel constipated? This is your first chakra in action.
- A recent breakup with your partner is the cause of a huge discomfort in your heart. This may be your fourth chakra calling!

Do you notice the connection here?

This can surely mean a lot if you begin to utilize this information in order to harmonize your emotions, enhance your health and well-being, feel more powerful, elevate your relationships, enhance your spiritual life, and gain an understanding of who you really are.

There are seven major chakras that are present along the midline of your body, starting from the base of your spine and going to the crown of your head. These chakras can also be called your "energy transformers," as they can transform or transport the energy present in the universe into your body via your energy centers.

Understanding chakras can accelerate the process of achieving holistic happiness and self-realization. Chakras can gift you your template for life, which can then be used as a barometer to measure your internal weather condition. In general, the first chakra provides you the will to survive. The second chakra helps you understand that now that you want to live, what you should do with your life—your immediate purpose. The third chakra provides guidance on how to achieve the purpose of life. The fourth chakra makes you aware of how you share the benefits of your achievements with others, how you love, and how you experience joy. The fifth chakra enables you to express your true self. The sixth chakra allows you to connect your material reality with your mental and spiritual aspirations. The seventh chakra aligns your relationship with a greater power or the infinite universe.

Chakras are said to be metaphysical in nature. They can serve as excellent examples of your decision-making abilities as well as the pattern in which you choose to make decisions.

Your chakras can be instrumental in bringing about a transformation in your personality; by harnessing the power of chakras, you may begin to believe in the possibility of achieving things that actually seem to be unthinkable at times!

The key here is your understanding of your chakras. Once you develop an understanding of each and every facet of your chakras, including what they represent and how they can be altered to achieve what you want, then you develop the power to heal yourself completely and create greater harmony and peace in your life.

Why do we call them chakras?
The word *chakra* is derived from an Proto-Indo-European word and implies "circle of wheel."

In ancient times, the word *chakra* was used to describe various circular things. The meaning of the term *chakra* has evolved through thousands of years. Today we use this word in the context of spinning circular wheels.

Here are some characteristics of chakras:

- No physical attributes are associated with chakras; however, they are considered as the parts of your nonphysical or energy body.
- Locating your chakras can enable you to locate the energy centers in your body.
- Most energy centers are sandwiched in between two sides. These can be called the exact location of the chakra.
- All chakras contain a number of petals, which represent a collection of energies. Colloquially we say that one chakra represents an energy, but actually each chakra is an energy system. The petals of the chakras symbolize all the energies in this system.

- Chakras are usually associated with colors, deities, elements, and mantras.

A Brief Look at the Seven Chakras

The first chakra

The first chakra is often referred to as your foundation chakra, earth chakra, or the root chakra. The root chakra possesses the qualities of Lord Ganesha, who is the Lord of all beginnings.

The Sanskrit term used for this chakra is the *muladhara chakra*.

In Sanskrit, *mula* means root, and *adharaa* means foundation. Therefore, *muladhara* means your root or basic foundation.

The muladhara chakra is located near the base of your spine, close to the pubic bone. It faces down toward your feet.

Earth is the symbolic element for this chakra, and the astral color of this chakra is red.

Since this chakra is nearest to the ground, it becomes the center of your feelings related to safety, survival, and security. We can say that this chakra lays the foundation of your entire body, and this could be one of the reasons for naming it as the root chakra.

When your muladhara chakra is open and healthy, you feel connected to the earth. This ensures that you are immensely comfortable in your skin and always feel safe. A strong self-confidence and great physical health are both signs of a harmonized and balanced root chakra.

You feel flighty or nongrounded when your muladhara chakra is closed or tight. In such a scenario, you generally possess a tendency to get influenced by your emotions. This leads to that lost feeling where you begin to feel that you do not belong anywhere.

People with a closed muladhara chakra generally have trouble managing even the basic aspects of their lives. Quite often, they do not practice healthy habits. It may lead to distractions that may become so strong that you forget to complete your basic duties, such as paying your bills, washing your face, brushing your teeth, or consuming dinner on time. Such individuals tend to fall down or slip quite a lot. They are also faced with difficulties in practicing basic yoga postures. The most common symptom in individuals with a weak root chakra is hip pain or foot pain. Such people also possess the tendency to twist their ankles.

A blocked muladhara chakra may lead to fear, procrastination, and defensiveness in an individual. It may also lead to development of suicidal tendencies in a person.

What should be your ultimate goal then?

It should be to try to balance your first chakra in a manner that it stays healthy and strong along with the other six chakras. This is important since the other six chakras stand on top of this chakra.

Many times we begin to believe that spirituality is much more important than our physical attributes. This prevents us from nurturing the first chakra.

From my perspective, it is important to understand that without a solid foundation of the first chakra, it may become extremely difficult to nurture your other chakras.

If I were to analyze your current situation, I would say that you stay in a world, you stay in a physical body, and you must attempt to do this in the best possible manner. A balanced muladhara chakra can provide you with the power and the resources to accomplish this. The fight-or-flight response in your body is accredited to this chakra.

The second chakra

The second chakra is also referred to as the sacral chakra or the hara chakra or, simply, the abdomen chakra. The Japanese practice of hara-kiri refers to the region of this chakra. This chakra possesses the qualities of Lord Prajapati, who is said to be the creator of new ideas.

In Sanskrit, it is called the *svadhisthana*. *Sva,* in Sanskrit means "of self," and *adhishthana* means "resting upon" or "abode." The word *adhastha* also means "inferior."

Therefore, this chakra is where your lower self generally rests. I also describe this chakra as a worldly person's ego drive; it drives the immediate goals that will satisfy the ego. The ego likes instant gratification.

The abdomen chakra is also the chakra of self-acceptance. A balanced chakra allows you to accept yourself as you are. It allows you to adapt to changes in your life.

This chakra is located in between the very base of your spinal column and navel. Orange is the astral color, and water is the symbolic element associated with this chakra.

The svadhisthana serves as the focal point for your feelings, creativity, emotions, sexuality, and movement. It is important to understand here that the feelings of love and kindness find their origin in the fourth chakra. However, the second chakra is associated with feelings of passion, desire, sexual relationships, and sexual attraction. It is this chakra that empowers women to create life. Your creative self also emerges from this chakra. This chakra is about your immediate objectives and desires; anything that satisfies an average ego falls under this chakra.

You tend to feel comfortable about your self-image and your emotions when your svadhisthana is strong, open, and healthy. It does not let your emotions overpower you. It also helps you remain unfazed from negative opinions of people about who you are and what you should be doing or not doing. You develop an ability to appreciate and accept change with ease. You begin to nurture your creative self. You can also get things done the way you want or make them happen the way you want.

What happens when this chakra is closed or out of balance?

In such a scenario, you may be confused about what your immediate purpose of life is. Your most painful questions may be "What am I doing?" Or "What should I do next?" You may be emotionally weak and suffer from guilt and depression. People who know you begin to perceive you as cold since you feel emotionally cutoff. There is also a chance that you are overly critical of your current state in terms of your physical body or your emotional, mental, or financial state.

The location of this chakra makes it govern your sexual organs, liver, gonad gland, stomach, kidney, upper intestine, gall bladder, spleen, adrenal glands, and middle spine.

Health issues may demonstrate as fertility problems, chronic pelvic pain, sexual issues, gynecological disorders, or prostate cancer.

If you experience some level of difficulty in bringing a task to a logical conclusion, feel detached from your creativity, or experience sexuality-related concerns, it is all a result of your blocked svadhisthana, crying for help.

A number of individuals struggle to lose weight, and no matter what they do, they do not seem to shrink that waistline. This may simply be a result of your blocked svadhisthana. You actually gain that extra fat to protect your sensitive sacral chakra.

I have noticed that when I am spiritually healing very complex cases of deep-rooted blocks in the "healees," if there is karmic sharing required, my own sacral chakra heats up, and my weight increases during the healing assignment. Once the healing assignment is complete, the weight starts becoming normal again. During healing assignments dealing with clearing up blocks to the immediate purpose(s) of life and self-acceptance, the heat of the energy generated in my svadhistanaa chakra is sometimes so much that my metal belt buckle becomes too hot to touch!

What happens when this chakra is wide open?

A wide open svadhisthana allows your passionate emotions to take control over you. This often prevents you from getting things done. You begin to feel too strongly about certain things, and this becomes an obstacle in your path to achieve something. You may also become a victim of several addictions—to sex, alcohol, and so on.

Have you heard of people who are too involved in sex and do not seem to demonstrate any emotional involvement? This is due to an imbalanced svadhisthana.

Balancing your first chakra can enable you to harmonize your second chakra too! A strong foundation leads to a great deal of emotional security.

THE THIRD CHAKRA

The third chakra is also called the abundance chakra or the solar chakra. The Sanskrit name for this chakra is manipura, and this is regarded as your seat of the power to achieve.

In Sanskrit, *mani* means "gem," and *pura* can mean a fortress, castle, or city. Therefore, *manipura* indicates the city of gems. All achievements—whether they are intellectual, social, or financial in nature—can be manifested from this chakra.

Most of the Vedic mantras energize this chakra in one way or another. This is the seat of the goddess *Gayatri*. The quintessential *Gayatri* mantra is associated with this chakra; chanting the *Gayatri* mantra makes the solar chakra resplendent with golden light. All the metaphysical powers, called *siddhis* in Yoga, can be achieved through the expansion and energizing of this chakra.

The associated element is fire, and the associated astral color for this chakra is sunny yellow.

This chakra is located in your stomach just above the navel and is related to your power of digestion. The transformation of food to energy happens in this chakra.

It is often said that you radiate out to the world whatever you take inside your body. This is because whatever you take inside gets converted into *pranic* energy and enables radiance through the solar plexus.

Individuals with a strong manipura project the radiance of sun, emerging from their third chakra.

An individual feels powerless in case his or her third chakra is closed; such an individual is generally left to the mercy of fate and has no control over the happenings around him or her. This leads to lack of willpower, and such individuals suffer from a victim mentality. They are usually ineffective and nonimpactful.

Digestive problems such as constipation, indigestion, and irritable bowel syndrome also originate in the manipura. A poor appetite, along with lack of interest in food, is accounted to a blocked third chakra. Unexplained weight gain is often experienced when your body tries to protect the manipura chakra.

If you are extremely strict with yourself and the people around you, self-centered, bossy, and overaggressive, it may be a sign of your overly active third chakra. Some people seem to be too loud and dominant, and the energy level that they possess enables them to take over the entire room. This is a symbol of a wide open manipura chakra. These individuals quite often tend to achieve whatever they want to, sometimes at the expense of other people. People can sometimes become overdominant due to the immense power that their solar chakra possesses.

The lure of this *chakra*—on both the material plane as well as the astral plane—is so intense that it causes you to not progress on to the higher chakras. Since this chakra has the nature of fire, whatever you put in it, it burns it and then asks for more. For example, this chakra sends you on a never-ending pursuit of status in life; when you are a manager in your job, it drives you to become a senior manager; when you become a senior manager with great effort, this chakra makes you feel as if nothing has been accomplished and it demands more accomplishment, so then you persevere to become a director or a vice president; this cycle doesn't end, and it doesn't let you sleep in peace even if you become a CEO after making great sacrifices. I have met a few CEOs in my career—very hardworking and smart individuals—but unfortunately, most of them said that they still felt unfulfilled and vulnerable in their current positions.

In India, I met some pundits with trained solar chakras who had hundreds of yogic scriptures learned by heart. They could recite them verse by verse with accuracy, but alas, they had no direct experience of what they were reciting about because their awareness had not expanded to the experiential level of the third eye or the crown chakra.

An unbalanced solar chakra draws the power of your soul and makes you burn and burn till you are done!

Anyway, you can emerge as a strong and confident individual who does not step on anybody else if you balance your manipura chakra. This enables you to follow your intuitions and also provides you a sense of who you really are. I would say that a balanced third chakra is a mix of courage, power, and humility—all combined together!

The Fourth Chakra

The fourth chakra is also called the heart chakra. The Sanskrit name for this chakra is *anahata*. In Sanskrit, *anahata* means "unhurt" or "unstruck."

At a tangible level, the name suggests that our heart should be made so strong that it remains unhurt or unscathed during all the trials and tribulations of life. At a deeper level, the name *anahata* refers to the *anahata naad* or the "unstruck sound" that you can hear in your right ear or the center of your head when your awareness has entered this energy center. This is the astral sound of silence; it is the real sound of aum, which cannot be imitated in words or created by any striking of a physical instrument. A majority of the Reiki raja-yoga initiates who are initiated to the third level of initiation are able to experience this sound. This sound of silence stays with them throughout and, in fact, becomes a meditation in itself. It is said that when you start hearing this unstruck sound, you have understood the essence of all the *Vedas* and other spiritual books. All the *Vedas* have emerged from this, the real sound of aum. The Sufis call this sound the **saut-e-sarmadi**.

The symbolic element for the heart chakra is air, and the astral colors are pink and green. As the name suggests, this chakra is located near your heart. The anahata chakra draws joy from the universe from the back and projects love from the front. Therefore, clairvoyantly, one can see energies of green color enter from the back of the heart chakra and project as pink energies of love from the front of the chakra.

Here is another interesting fact about this chakra: this chakra is the middle chakra. The three chakras below it are all worldly chakras; the lower three chakras define your lower self. The three chakras above the heart chakra are all increasingly spiritual chakras; they define the higher self. The heart chakra acts as a connection between these two sides. It is this chakra that ensures that your worldly propensities are balanced with your spiritual qualities. It, therefore, enables you to enjoy a spiritual life along with the physical life!

These two components—spirituality and physical life—live together because of love, and this is the fuel for life!

The heart chakra is the seat of the energies of Lord Vishnu riding the celestial phoenix Garuda. Garuda devours the snakes of doubts, pessimism, and depression. The heart chakra can reach from one point to another at the speed of air, which is the element of the heart chakra.

The love projected from the heart chakra can reach anywhere in this space and time, like the mighty Garuda. Of course, this mighty Garuda is ridden by Lord Vishnu himself, who represents the power that keeps this universe in balance. Therefore, the role of the heart chakra is to keep our lower two chakras (lower self) in balance with the two higher chakras (higher self).

Many years back when during a meditation, my consciousness fully ascended to the heart center, and I had a beatific vision of Lord Vishnu on the mighty Garuda. Having a scientific background, I certainly do not meditate to see visions, but in this case the vision was spontaneous, all engrossing, undeniable, and heavenly beautiful. It transformed me immediately with a feeling of joy, relief, fulfillment, and spiritual assurance that has stayed with me since then. My guru used to say that in meditation, the vision is not as important, even meditation itself is not as important; what is important is what becomes of you after the vision. Who you become from inside out after the meditation is what's important. There are thousands of books written on visions and meditation techniques; most of them talk about relaxation or the ability to see the aura or the Divine, but very few of them talk about inner transformation. The path of Reiki raja-yoga transforms you from inside through a series of nondenominational spiritual practices. You no longer remain your older unanchored self, floating in this world like a leaf in the wind; there is connection established with this universe and its Absolute power that holds you anchored in tough times and doesn't let you forget your spiritual aim in the pleasurable moments. This is the power of Reiki raja-yoga.

The heart chakra is also the seat of John the Baptist.

Your relationships may get impacted and you may experience trouble loving somebody in case your fourth chakra is closed. The shallowness that you sometimes experience in your love life, the lack of empathy and compassion that you feel, could all be a result of your closed or shrinking anahata. This may sometimes go to such an extent that you may stop loving yourself.

The heart chakra is the energy center where, after learning Reiki raja-yoga, you can experience unconditional love for the first time. This unconditional love is Reiki. During the Reiki practice, an intoxicating all-engrossing feeling takes you over; its origination and destination cannot be found. It is just there and brings about profound healing at multiple levels of your being. This feeling is the feeling of unconditional love flowing from the Absolute to your heart chakra.

In my practice, I have observed that sometimes an overuse of lower chakras draws energies from the heart chakra, causing a lack of love in the subject's life and, in extreme cases, may result in a heart attack. In the latter case, people may be so focused on work and material accomplishments that they may draw energy from all their higher chakras into their lower chakras. They may have no time to enjoy and be thankful for what they already have; this will lead to blocks in the heart chakra that, when left unchecked, may take a pathological form and may cause blockages in the arteries of the physical heart. There are, at best, very limited ways to medically validate what I am saying. However, according to Reiki, negative blocks first arise in your thoughts, then they manifest as energy blocks in your chakras and aura, and eventually, undetected by routine medical instruments, the blocks then take a physical form, which is when traditional medicine is able to diagnose them. In many cases, this is too late. Medical science will eventually catch up and be able to detect disease in its energy, or better still, in its thought stage.

Let me now ask you to imagine for a moment the feeling that you could get if your fourth chakra were closed when the third one was open.

If such a scenario arose, all you might care about would be success and power. In this case, life could just be about your own self, and you might just not care about anybody else.

This is the reason why a closed fourth chakra can lead to heart diseases, angina attacks, clogged arteries, and so on.

A number of poses in yoga focus on opening this center of energy simply because it is the linking chakra between your physical and spiritual self. Backbend yoga poses are really helpful in balancing the anahata. The thymus gland, hands, lungs, heart, and arms are associated with this chakra.

And *how about a really wide open anahata?*

That may lead you to develop a martyr mind-set; you become immensely focused on helping others and completely forget about yourself. This leads you to lose that sense of personal power of grounding because all that you are concerned about is giving away. The feelings of empathy may become so strong in your system that you may lose your actual identity and feelings.

The answer to loving deeply, fully, and sincerely lies in balancing the anahata. This quality to love yourself and others can bring an immense sense of compassion and inner peace.

This chakra is actually the key link in a long chain leading up to a connection with the divine heart.

The fifth chakra

Another name for the fifth chakra is the throat chakra. In Sanskrit, this chakra is often referred to as *vishuddha*. *Vishuddha* means "completely pure." This refers to the purity that emerges in your being after going through the grinding wheels of the experiences of the four chakras below the throat chakra. After your lower chakras have been refined and after you have started experiencing unconditional love, a new you starts to emerge. This new self of yours has an innate understanding of the law of karma and thus develops patience and equanimity under all circumstances. Your awareness at this chakra is the beginning of the deep dive that is about to happen in the infinite ocean of calmness, stillness, and peace.

The throat chakra is the seat of Lord Shiva as the *Neelkanth*. The legend is that during the epic churning of the ocean, in addition to the unheard-of treasures, many lethal impurities came out. These poisonous impurities, if not consumed by a higher power, had the destructive power to destroy our planet. Lord Shiva, who was meditating in the Himalayas, stood up for all the sentient beings—including the deities, demons, and humankind—and drank that poison to prevent it from destroying the earth. The effect of the poison was so strong that his throat turned blue, but he didn't let the poison reach and affect his heart. The moral of the story is that in your normal course of life, you go through so many negative experiences. These negative experiences take a toll on you, converting your otherwise loving self into a bitter and brooding person. Your throat chakra has the power of patience and understanding to bear the brunt of the negativities that some ignorant people in your life hurl at you and nullify their effect without letting it affect your heart and sullying your ability to freely express yourself. The throat chakra, therefore, is the power of patience, understanding, and self-expression. It also serves as the bridge between the feelings of the heart chakra and the rationality of the third eye.

The symbolic element for the fifth chakra is the sky or space. The astral color is bright sapphire blue, which evokes the awareness of infinite space inviting you to expand into it. A yogi-healer who has evolved into the awareness of the throat chakra can make his or her presence felt across space and can send spiritual vibrations through great distances.

The vishuddha is associated with your inborn capability to express, judge, communicate, and create. The parts of the body that are connected with the fifth chakra are the parathyroid and the thyroid gland, arms, hands, neck, and shoulders.

This chakra enables you to produce your voice.

Many times we are faced with situations wherein we need to express our thoughts and just don't seem to get enough words to do so. Everything is there in the mind; however, the structure seems to be missing. In this case, try drawing or writing your thoughts on a piece of paper. You may just be surprised with the outcome—thanks to your fifth chakra. It will enable you to write down your thoughts in the most logical and clear manner—in the manner that you want to speak.

The vishuddha is often referred to as the truth center—it empowers you to speak and hear the truth. It is also said that if you have never used this chakra to utter a lie, then whatever you say will come true. While it is hard to test this claim, it is true that when your awareness evolves into this chakra, your words do become powerful, and in due course of time, whatever you say with focus and intensity manifests partially or fully.

You may face trouble communicating with others in case your fifth chakra is closed. In such a situation, you may stammer, stumble over words, or simply try to maintain silence even when it is appropriate to speak.

Sometimes you just know what you want to say, but there is something that prevents those words from coming out of your throat. You develop fear of speech and often swallow your thoughts. This is your closed vishuddha, calling for attention.

A closed fifth chakra can also make you a compulsive liar. In fact, you may begin to lie to yourself by trying to convince yourself that whatever you are saying is the truth.

You may begin to suffer from creative blocks and not be able to find your inspiration. Talking about your health, a closed throat chakra can mean diseases such as sore throat, laryngitis, ear infection, or neck pain.

Sometimes when you want to say something, words don't seem to get out of your throat, and you experience a lump right there in your throat.

What happens when your vishuddha is open too wide?

Well, you may just become a chatterbox. In this case, you begin to speak too much and experience trouble listening to others.

Some people tend to argue continually; they try to take control of the situation, always trying to prove their point, without caring about the sentiments of other people. These people generally have a wide open vishuddha.

And what would happen in case your fourth chakra were closed but the fifth one was wide open? This could make you so much inclined toward intellectual talking that in reality you might lack compassion, even toward activities occurring right under your nose.

If you focus on balancing the throat chakra, you can develop the power to tap into the heart chakra below and use the power of intuition above in order to speak and hear just the truth. In this scenario, you become magnetized with creative energy and are immensely sensitive toward the needs of others.

This also enhances the process of purification of ideas and transformation of things around you.

THE SIXTH CHAKRA

The sixth chakra is also called the brow chakra or the third-eye chakra. It is referred to as *ajna* in Sanskrit. *Ajna* means command.

It signifies self-knowledge or spiritual genius. In the Hindu scripture the *Bhagavad Gita*, the character of Lord Shri Krishna represents this spiritual genius. Shri Krishna was the ruler of mathura. *Mathura* esoterically means the area of the forehead. He was the friend, philosopher, and guide of the righteous warrior Arjuna. Arjuna represents the ideal seeker—a fearless yet principled material achiever, a go-getter, with complete faith in the Absolute and the guru.

Reiki raja-yoga encourages you to become like Arjuna, who is guided by the spiritual genius of the sixth chakra.

In a spiritually evolved person, the third-eye chakra is the command center of the mind and the body. Opening of this chakra leads to spiritual genius, as compared to the solar chakra, which turns you into a material genius.

The astral color associated with this chakra is deep indigo. Deep royal purple is also a color associated with this chakra when the awareness starts progressing into the higher energies of this chakra in its movement toward the crown chakra. The symbolic element for this chakra is *para-akash* or beyond space. You can also consider light as the symbolic element for this chakra.

This chakra is also called the center of your self-knowledge and intuition.

Sometimes before something happens, you come to know about it. You can figure out what will happen even if you lack physical evidence to support your thoughts. Sometimes your conscious mind is unable to detect certain things that exist. These can be detected by your power of intuition—the sixth chakra.

The ajna fills you with inner knowledge about the world and about your own self. The skills of perception, knowing, and questioning are all associated with this chakra. This chakra is also the storehouse of your dreams and aspirations.

Self-doubt is the most common malady that affects a person with a blocked third eye. You may become oblivious about your own inner intelligence in case your sixth chakra or the ajna is closed. Sometimes you may experience an urge to seek support from a friend, accept a particular job opportunity, or discuss a long-pending issue with your partner, and your closed third eye does not let you respond to those urges. In the process, you begin to ignore these urges. You spend most of the time in your body or the physical life, and then there is absolutely no time left for nurturing the inner sixth sense.

An overburdened sixth chakra may also lead you to experience health problems such as sinus headaches, nearsightedness, tension headaches, and other problems of the eye.

And what happens if the ajna is wide open?

A wide open *ajna* may lead you to just ignore the needs of others. Your capability to judge things is generally clouded by your emotions, and you almost never get to witness the big picture.

You may also become ungrounded and overly intellectual and begin to think too much about everything. You may start believing that your dreams are a reality and get captivated in spiritual search or psychic seeing. Sometimes when you begin to view yourself simply as a soul, you begin to ignore the needs of your physical body.

If you are spending loads of time in meditation and neglecting life's other duties, you need to work upon your lower chakras.

The other retrogressive trait of the overactive third-eye chakra is jealousy. You will find that two people who have overactive *third-eye chakras* will never truly agree with each other. They will both have their own theories about how the world works, the origin and purpose of life, and what is God. This world has no shortage of fitness gurus, management gurus, financial gurus, yoga gurus, spiritual gurus, and so on, and each has his or her own theory. If you ever get a chance to observe their behavior, you will find that the ones with overactive third-eye chakras will always be jealous of one another. An overactive third eye cannot stand another overactive third eye, the same as two swords cannot stay in the same sheath!

A balanced ajna enables you to tap into your inner knowledge and builds your focus so that you remain grounded in the body and in the world. Ultimately, this harmony helps you balance your strong intellect with feelings about people around you.

This is a good point to mention that a higher chakra can also heal the lower chakras—the same as an elder brother can heal the younger brothers (or sisters).

Here's how this happens.

Will to live at the root chakra can be found if you have a purpose of life at the abdomen chakra. The purpose of life can be ignited by the pursuit of knowledge and abundance of the solar chakra. Our need to give and receive love and joy in the heart chakra guides us to acquire knowledge that can benefit others and abundance that can be shared. "You can only give what you have."

To overcome the obstacles you encounter on your journey from root or abdomen to solar and heart requires the patience and the coherent self-expression of the throat chakra. All this needs to be accomplished without losing sight of the spiritual aspect of life—the connection between physical and mental accomplishments, with spiritual progress monitored by the third-eye chakra.

Now here is another interesting fact. My guru once told me that in the higher order of yogis, the ajna chakra is also, secretly, referred to as the *agyan* chakra. In Hindi, *agyan* means "ignorance." In Sanskrit, too, the root word *ajJa* means "ignorant." This is because ignorance, in the subtlest but the most harmful form, manifests at this chakra. When the yogi experiences his newfound mastery of all the lower five chakras, he has developed self-control and self-acceptance. He also experiences pure joy, develops precise self-expression, and gains a level of self-realization. In this state of almost holistic happiness, he then starts thinking he is God! He then starts propounding his own philosophies and his own spiritual theories, starts founding new religions, amasses a following, and starts calling himself God. This is the subtlest form of ignorance—like a wall of glass—that keeps him away from true enlightenment, sometimes for lifetimes. Many such third-eye chakra yogis retrogress to lower chakras after repeatedly going against the karmic law and other spiritual laws of the Divine. Some of them become puppets in the hands of their followers; these followers praise them for their miracles, and the poor "God-men" have to find new tricks and *siddhis* to entertain their followers. What a pity!

At the third-eye chakra, when destiny becomes more or less in your control and holistic happiness is yours to enjoy, you have to remember one word—*surrender*. Surrender to the Absolute—wholeheartedly and with unflinching faith—is the only way to moksha, nirvana, or enlightenment. It takes more than 100 percent physical, mental, and spiritual effort to get to the ajna chakra—the command center. But then you still need to completely surrender to realize and integrate with the Absolute in the crown chakra.

THE SEVENTH CHAKRA

The seventh chakra is also referred to as the thousand-petaled lotus chakra or the crown chakra. This is called *sahasrara* in Sanskrit. I call this chakra the chakra of a thousand lights; each light represents an evolution of our awareness into self-realization.

This chakra is the seat of the formless consciousness—the supreme Almighty—where all chakras become one; the multiple states of intelligences of different chakras merge into one integrated consciousness. Yoga thus happens.

The astral colors of this chakra form a gradient from purple to white to a lightless light. This lightless light is a spiritual light that lights all the other lights in this universe; it cannot be described effectively in words. The closest that you can come to understanding it without direct experience is that there is a presence; you realize that this is an unbroken connected presence in everything and everywhere. The symbolic element for this chakra is pure awareness; you become increasingly aware of that Absolute that cannot be described in words.

In more definable terms, the sahasrara is your seat of wisdom, enlightenment, or pure consciousness. *Your universal self is greater than you; it goes much beyond your physical self and is seated in the crown chakra.*

A balanced and healthy seventh chakra implies a healthy spiritual life. The awareness that connects you with all things is a result of your balanced sahasrara. *You communicate with the Absolute though this chakra.*

A closed seventh chakra indicates that you do not have interest in any kind of spiritual pursuit.

A closed seventh chakra also implies that you do not believe in spiritual healing through chakras. Since you picked up this book, it is likely that you do not have a closed crown chakra. However, there may be times when you experience a momentary shutdown in the seventh chakra; this can be your chakra responding to a physical crisis, isolation, depression, death of a loved one, or any other personal tragedy.

A wide open seventh chakra may lead you to enjoy a solitary life and spiritual pursuits. For example, such people often enjoy living all by themselves in the Himalayas.

Your aim should be to balance your seventh chakra along with the other six chakras. A balanced crown chakra would mean that you are grounded and also possess a sense of spirituality that makes you believe in your connectedness with the things around you.

The practice of Reiki raja-yoga harmonizes the multiple intelligences of all chakras. These intelligences blend into one, and Yoga is achieved. The yogi becomes spontaneous; only necessary vrittis or thoughts arise in his or her mind, and they arise not out of selfish desire but as guidance from the divine will and divine grace. In a Japanese Buddhist sense, a state of *shibumi* is achieved—a state of effortless perfection.

Meditation becomes existence, and all existence becomes meditation; mindfulness and empty-mindedness become one. You become what is needed of you. You still have the will to live of the root chakra, the goals of the abdomen chakra, the abundance of the solar chakra, the love and joy of the heart chakra, the patience and understanding and its self-expression of the throat chakra, and the spiritual genius of the third-eye chakra—but all of these don't bind or define you; they all blend in one awareness. The purpose of Reiki raja-yoga is thus fulfilled.

In my sessions, people sometimes discuss their thoughts related to chakras and the impact they have on us. Some of the things that I have heard are pure myths and must be clarified:

- *Myth one*: Chakras are the cause of and solution to each and every problem.

  Fact: Your problems are given by your karma and not by your chakras. Chakras project energies based on your vrittis, samakaras, and sankalpas—remember, you read about them earlier! A number of people start blaming their first chakra whenever they feel ungrounded. You must understand that chakras enable you to understand your energy condition better so that you can perform karma or actions that are beneficial for you. So, if you want to ground yourself, you must consume healthy food, visit home in case you have been staying away from family, manage your finances better, and also meditate to balance your first chakra. Since chakras are not the only cause of your problems, just balancing them will not be the panacea to all your problems. Your practical karma (actions), vrittis (thoughts), chitta (subconscious mind), samskaras (mental impressions), and sankalpas (limiting concepts), along with your aura, need to be addressed as well. Reiki and raja-yoga techniques focus on your complete thought and energy system to achieve harmony within and outside you so that you can discover holistic happiness.

- *Myth two*: Chakras serve as the door to the harmful kundalini energy.

  Fact: In reality, the chakras protect you against this intense energy; they do not serve as facilitators. If you perform spiritual practice under an authentic master, your chakras only open up when you are ready to take this energy. In all other situations, they may remain closed, like a valve. Haphazard practice and techniques picked up from here and there can cause kundalini energy to rise abruptly and cause "tears" in the overloaded chakras. Therefore, proper practice under an experienced master is critical.

- *Myth three*: The first chakra elevates the animal instinct in you and makes you wild.

  Fact: The first chakra is the grounding chakra; it is not wild. Balancing the first chakra ensures that you do not lose control over your senses and stay calm and peaceful.

- *Myth four:* The second chakra is about sex only.

  Fact: The second chakra has a lot to do with passion, pleasure, creativity, and things that you love to do, not just sex.

- *Myth five*: The third chakra is a "bad" chakra.

  Fact: No, the third chakra is not a bad chakra. In fact, no chakra is bad. You have to use the willpower of achievement in a positive manner. Reiki raja-yoga practices are based on the philosophy that love should guide your willpower and your willpower should be full of love.

- *Myth six*: The fourth chakra is only about loving and nurturing others.

  Fact: While loving others is an important ability of the fourth chakra, it has more to do with loving and healing yourself along with loving others.

- *Myth seven*: The fifth chakra is all about communicating to the outside world.

  Fact: I would say, yes and no, simply because your fifth chakra is also about your properly grasping the world communicating back to you. Communication is about expressing as well as about receiving and processing.

- *Myth eight*: The sixth chakra is only associated with psychic power.

  Fact: This may be true for some people but is usually irrelevant for most. It has more to do with the power of your intuition and being aware of your higher self.

- *Myth nine*: The seventh chakra is about God.

  Fact: You do not have to believe in any particular faith or God to harness the power of your seventh chakra. It is more about your connection with a higher power or the Absolute, depending on how it makes sense to you.

In addition to auras and chakras, an aspiring Reiki raja-yogi (hopefully you!) should also familiarize himself or herself with a few additional yogic concepts—life-force energy, *nadis,* mantras, and *prema*.

THE CONCEPT OF LIFE-FORCE ENERGY

The Sanskrit term used for life-force energy is *prana*. This is the energy that flows in and out of your body. In fact, it flows in and out of every living thing.

Do not confuse prana with breath, as prana rides on the breath. You may want to call breath a vehicle that helps in transport of prana in and out of your body. Balancing this prana can lead to an overall harmonious body and mind that has the capability to heal itself—physically, mentally, emotionally, and spiritually!

The Chinese use the term *qi* or *chi* for life-force energy. This implies that chi is also life-force energy, just like prana. It is called *gi* in Korean, *khi* in Vietnamese, and *ki* in Japanese.

HOW DOES THIS PRANA TRAVEL INTO YOUR BODY?

The prana flows in and out of the body through the chakras and *nadis* or channels of energy. *Nadi* is the Sanskrit name for channels of energy. The Chinese refer to these as meridians of energy. The chakras, as you have read earlier, are vortices of energy inside your body.

One of the most important channels of energy in your body is the *sushumna nadi,* which begins at your first chakra and ends at your seventh chakra. It pierces through the center of each chakra. It travels from the base of your spine to the crown of your head. It divides into two parts when it reaches your sixth chakra. The first part moves up to the seventh chakra in a straight line. The second part travels in a curved line along the back side of your brain and joins with the first part at the seventh chakra.

This is considered extremely important, as this is the *nadi* that carries your kundalini energy from the base of the spine to the crown of the head.

There are two other *nadis* that wrap themselves around the sushumna nadi. They are called the *ida* and the *pingala nadis* and are present around each chakra.

You must have heard about the Chinese concept of yin and yang energy. It is identical to *ida* and *pingala*. Ida is the cooling, calm, receptive, and meditative energy that can also be called the female or the lunar energy. Pingala is your heating, active, forceful, energetic energy. You need it when you want to get something done.

Breathing out of your left nostril helps you channelize your ida's energy. Breathing out of your right nostril helps you channelize your pingala's energy. Ida carries the yin energy, and pingala carries the yang energy. *Pranayama* exercises, as taught in Reiki raja-yoga, can fill your body with prana energy and help in tapping into your ida and pingala energy too.

It is also important to note that ida energy can calm an overloaded chakra and pingala energy can energize a blocked chakra. Ida energy is said to be good for calming exercises, whereas the pingala energy is great for energizing exercises.

Here I would also like to talk about *antahkarana*. The difference between *antahkarana* and *sushumna* is key and is not well-known. *Antahkarana* is the pillar of light that descends from the source into our crown and envelops the *sushumna*. Reiki descends through the antahkarana.

Antahkarana is the link between your ego-personality and your highest self. Some philosophers refer to it as the bridge of consciousness between the highest spirit and the lowest matter. It is composed of five strands of energy. Out of this, two strands are created by the higher self, and three strands are projected upward in the consciousness by you. It is important that these strands are consciously built by you. This makes you a conscious creator.

Kundalini, on the other hand, ascends through the sushumna. Here again, my realization is that *sushumna* stands for *sukshma* or "subtle" and *mana* or "mind."

Some people acquire the ability to see their own chakras through the power of meditation. They tend to notice energy vortices moving clockwise or anticlockwise. They may also notice certain disturbances. Your chakras change their size, shape, and spinning speed throughout the day. They work in a manner that your prana moves inside them; they utilize it to their full potential and then release it back into the universe. This is similar to an energy transformer.

But there are times when things may not go your way and changes may occur inside your chakras. Temporary changes generally do not lead to any major harm. The problem arises with chronic changes. That is when you will need to balance your chakras and ensure that they become healthy and balanced again.

THE RELATIONSHIP BETWEEN CHAKRAS AND MINDFULNESS:
Mindfulness can empower you to experience your chakras. You may want to scan your energy body to notice how your chakras are moving

and acting. When you are mindful, you get a better perception of these chakras; you learn to feel them, measure them, and heal them.

Here is an exercise (I call this a complete brain workout) that you can practice in order to enhance your mindfulness:

- Sit comfortably with your spine erect. You can sit anywhere—on a yoga mat, a folded blanket, or a chair. The focus has to be on your spine; that has to be erect.
- Now, lower your eyes. Your eyes should be at a forty-five-degree angle, preferably half-closed and half-open. The key here is that you are practically not looking at anything.
- Don't try to stop your thoughts. They are thoughts; they will keep coming. Just observe them. You can visualize a thought as a gift wrapped up inside a piece of paper and just labeled as "thought."
- Now, make yourself aware of your physical body. Notice how your body feels. Let the power of mindfulness guide you to notice and feel each portion of your body. The right shoulder may hurt, and the tummy could feel bloated. Just do not get up and eat something. Concentrate on feeling each and every sensation. Visualize these sensations, wrap them up in a piece of paper, and label them "shoulder ache," "bloated tummy," and so on.
- Next, move to the room around you. I am not asking you to get up and move; I am simply asking you to be aware of the room around you. How does the air feel? Can you smell a particular aroma? Does the blanket feel warm? Once again, visualize all that you can feel and wrap it up in a piece of paper—"the aroma of chamomile tea," "cool breeze," and so on.
- Finally, come back to your awareness. Step away from your thoughts, from what you are feeling in your physical body, and from the things happening around you. Let them stay where

they are—wrapped up in pieces of paper but not disturbing you.
- Try to stay in this state for at least five minutes. Gradually increase the time to about twenty minutes each day.

How can the practice of mindfulness introduce you to your chakras?

You can open your chakras by just being mindful. Let me demonstrate this for you:

- Begin by lying down on the floor on a yoga mat. You should focus on tucking your shoulder blades under you. This is important as it makes your chest feel open and broad. Now, stretch your legs as far as you can and then relax them. Your arms should be placed about one foot from the sides of your body. The palms should be facing up.
- Next, try to get into the mindfulness mode. Detach from your thoughts. Do not try to stop the thoughts from occurring; just try to visualize them, wrap them up, label them, and move ahead, visualizing your physical body, surroundings, and awareness overall.
- Now that you are detached from your thoughts, you can start the process of awareness or mindfulness. You can begin by bringing your awareness to your first chakra. This means that you are being aware of the base of your spine and you are visualizing the round, red chakra that is turning like a wheel. You can feel it by just being mindful. Your thoughts may just come and go. Don't attempt to stop them; just be conscious about your chakra. Try to visualize your chakra and feel your chakra.
- The next step would be to shift your awareness toward your sacral chakra. This is your second chakra. It may appear like a spinning ball of energy that is orange in color. It is all right if you

- do not see it yet. Awareness is all about feeling it. Just feel it below your navel and make a mental note of your perceptions.
- Now, you must try to feel each chakra in its serial order—so, feel your third chakra right below your rib cage (this may appear yellow in color) and the fourth chakra in the center of your chest (this would be pink or green in color). Now shift your mindfulness to your fifth chakra, which is blue in color, and then to your sixth chakra, which may appear indigo in color. Lastly, feel your seventh chakra (which may be purple or white in color). Do not attempt to imagine your chakra; just try to feel them.
- Once you have felt all your chakras, move your toes and fingers a little; this is to bring your consciousness back to the physical world. Now, roll toward the right side and sit up when you feel ready.
- Grab a notebook and note down your experiences with chakras. Write down all that you experienced during the exercise. This is important because it will help you track any noticeable patterns with respect to chakras. You should also repeat this exercise at least once a week in order to get clarity on the patterns.

You may find this difficult in the beginning. Mindfulness exercises call for concentrating your conscious efforts on being aware. This can become challenging at times. I understand that you are now tempted to feel your chakras and encourage you to try this exercise. However, don't be disheartened if you are unable to perceive your energy centers at this time. It's all about trying at some other time and practicing mindfulness throughout the day. With focused efforts you will be able to tune in to your energy centers.

The mindfulness aspects of Reiki and raja-yoga can ensure that you achieve optimum balance and harmony within all your chakras.

Even a single blocked chakra may lead to an imbalance in the chakras. This may lead to an elevated level of stagnant energy in some areas of your life and a reduced energy level in certain other areas. The final impact may be poor health, unpleasant life circumstances, and lack of general well-being.

Is it possible to eradicate this blockage?

Absolutely.

You would have to begin by clearing your chakras through incorporating loads of positive changes in your life. And remember, all these changes must begin with your own self.

Has it ever happened that you have changed your occupation, wardrobe, and even your place of residence, and yet there seems to be something missing?

This "something missing" is a result of the chakra imbalance in your body. This necessarily means that you would have to work on healing yourself through healing your blocked chakras.

Some powerful strategies that can empower you to harmonize your life by bringing balance in your energy centers are:

Energy-healing techniques: Reiki is a proven technique in this category. Energy healers can assist you in opening up your chakras when they sense a blockage. Crystals, fine needles, gemstones, touch, or pressure and intention are some of the tools utilized by energy healers. Crystals are often identified based on the vibrations of the chakra to be balanced. Needles, touch, and pressure can work by providing a physical boost to your meridians. Love, intent, focused thoughts, and emotions are the most important factors in energy healing.

The process of Reiki healing mandates the transfer of the power of unconditional love into your body, which in turn works on the areas that need it the most.

Color therapy: You may just be in love with certain colors. They may appear to be relaxing and soothing. And then there may be some that may just make you feel bad about something. In fact, certain colors may even irritate you! Did you know that your relationship with color is also based on the state of your chakras? Colors possess unique qualities that can enable you to harmonize your chakras. The use of specific colors in the environment of clothing can help your blocked chakras. Color can also be utilized when you make choices related to food. Colorful vegetables and fruits may also help in balancing your chakras.

Sound therapy: Sound therapy uses the power of vibrations that your body can feel, along with the power of your intuition. Sometimes you want to listen to extremely loud music. This peps you up! And then, there are times when you want to hear something that is relaxing and calm. The key here is to go with what feels right to your body. Just follow your intuition. I would also encourage you to listen to recorded sounds of bells, chimes, Tibetan singing bowls, and so on.

Visualization: Visualization is considered one of the most impactful tools toward harmonizing your chakras. Memorizing the significance and functions of each chakra helps in positive visualization. Once you have understood and memorized this, you should visualize yourself as someone who has achieved perfection in each area. Your current situation may not allow that; you may be unwell, tired, guilty, unhappy, and so on. You should still endeavor to align your energy with things that you want to achieve; just visualize that you have already achieved those things. Do you want to achieve success, happiness, love, health, and general well-being? Visualize yourself as somebody who is super-successful; feel that each chakra is filling your body, mind, and soul with that ultimate energy. Let this power of visualization empower you to harness your greatest potential through the power of chakra balancing.

Positive affirmations: These are powerful chants, quotes, or mantras that encourage you to boost positive emotions. You can choose any powerful chant or mantra that you like. You may even create your own mantra. The key here is that your mantra should be strong enough to ignite positive emotions in your mind, body, and spirit. These affirmations can be used every day in your yoga or meditation practice. You can recite them aloud to yourself, packed with feelings and concentrated on the outcome that you wish to achieve. A simple positive affirmation sentence said thrice a day standing in front of the mirror can work wonders.

Raja-yoga: The practice of raja-yoga enables you to achieve optimum mental and physical balance. It can, therefore, be termed your inside-out approach to harmonize the chakras. It helps in achieving the perfect mind-body synchronization.

Breathing meditation: The simplest known tried-and-true methodology to achieve calm is through the use of breathing meditation. When you focus on your breath, you allow yourself to slow down your heart rate. This in turn empowers your mind and body to slow down. Want to achieve inner peace and tranquility at a moment's notice? The answer lies in breathing meditation!

Daily practice of some or all of these techniques, along with certain guided discipline techniques, can help balance and harmonize your life through balancing your chakras. And it is never too late to begin!

In the Reiki raja-yoga seminars that I conduct, I reveal certain highly potent techniques that are specifically designed to accelerate your progress toward mindfulness, chakra balancing, and holistic happiness. The practice of Reiki raja-yoga uses the best of all the healing strategies mentioned above in such an organized way that even the busiest person can practice them.

Bija Mantras

Bija mantras can be defined as the mantras that are chanted to open, heal, and harmonize your chakras. The word *bija* finds its roots in the Sanskrit language and means "seed" in English. This seed implants the most powerful energy inside your body. It ensures that each chakra aligns itself with the other chakras in your body. This helps you in achieving the desired state of harmony.

These bija mantras or seed mantras can be chanted as a series of mantras in order to strengthen your seven chakras. Alternatively, you may choose to chant one particular mantra in order to boost an individual chakra. You may choose to chant these in your mind or sing them aloud; it all depends on your preference. It must, however, be noted that mental chanting takes one deeper into the meditation than chanting out loud. Visualizing the color, location. and positive impact of each chakra as you chant the corresponding bija mantra can provide you an added dose of energy.

The process of repeating or remembering the mantra is termed *japa*. There is also a term called *ajapa-japa,* which implies constant awareness. The experience of *japa* without requiring any mental effort to recite the mantra is termed *ajapa-japa*. Here is a simple chakra chant meditation using the bija mantras:

- The process of chanting the bija mantra begins in the root chakra. Visualize the root chakra and recite the sound *lam*.
- Now, visualize your sacral chakra by reciting *vam*.

- Next, boost your solar plexus chakra through the chant of *ram*.
- Elevate your heart chakra now using the sound *yam*.
- Open your throat chakra by the chant of *ham*.
- Now, visualize and enhance your third-eye *chakra* with the sound of *om*.
- And finally, open your crown chakra through visualization and creating an extended sound of *om*. You can also maintain complete silence at this time.

Throughout this process, focus on visualizing loving and nurturing energy traveling through your body and into the universe. Use the power of affirmations to remind you that you can feel this positive energy—you can feel it travel from your root chakra to your crown chakra and then into the universe.

You will be amazed at the balance and harmony that you can achieve by simply practicing this chakra chant for a few minutes every day. And look at the element of flexibility. Given your busy lifestyle, you have the freedom to chant anywhere you want, anytime you want—during lunchtime, in your car, while doing the dishes, while baking and cooking, while folding your laundry, while walking or running, as a part of your meditation or yoga practice, while traveling, or even while bathing. All that it calls for is sincerity on your part.

You will be able to achieve and maintain perfect rhythm (good health and harmony) when you treat your body as a miraculous orchestra and then strive hard to maintain the harmony of the individual instruments in this orchestra (in this case, chakras).

Karmic blocks in aura and chakras in reality imply blocks in your life, since life is pretty much a reflection of your energy or aura. These karmic blocks lead to unhappiness.

The Power of Unconditional Love or Prema

Understanding the meaning of unconditional love makes it easier for us to share it.

Prema is a Hindi word that comes from the Sanskrit root *preman*. *Prema* fundamentally means unconditional love. It is the cornerstone of the Reiki raja-yoga philosophy. Reiki is nothing but unconditional love.

Unconditional love, prema, or Reiki is the controller of prana. I have already discussed prana earlier. Wherever Reiki is, prana is automatically balanced. Prana is *shakti* (will, self-effort); prema is the *bhakti* (devotion, surrender) that sustains that prana. They are both needed to achieve holistic happiness.

When we mention the term *unconditional love*, it implies *giving love without expecting something or anything in return.*

This kind of love does not measure the amount of love that should be given. It does not even ask if the person who is going to be receiving this love deserves it or not.

The prema or unconditional love emanating from our soul has a quality of being comforting, soothing, compassionate, and uplifting.

The soul has the power to offer such unconditional love without waiting for someone to reward, appreciate, acknowledge, or praise what he or she has just received. We all have souls; in fact, we are souls.

Therefore, it is only logical to say that each one of us has the potential to give out and share this unconditional love.

Reiki opens doors to accepting the fact that prema or pure unconditional love is present within us. This ability to love has been bestowed upon us by the Absolute by his power of grace (*kripa* in Sanskrit). Receiving this shining pure love can enable you to instantly surpass any pain. This can facilitate the healing process within you. By channeling unconditional love, you heal yourself physically, emotionally, and spiritually, which in turn can open up your mind in realizing your true self.

As you read through this book, it may sound easy to give and receive unconditional love. However, in reality, pouring the gift of prema or unconditional love on your least favorite person is way too hard, especially if you are not ready.

The single culprit that most divides humanity is lack of understanding. Try to take a break from this earthly reality, separate yourself from your physical being, think of yourself as a pure soul who has the ability to love without any conditions. Would you be able to live up to this?

Human nature adds conditions in whatever we do or give—no matter how small it may be. In order to attain your highest potential and create a happier world, it is really important to accept who you really are and the immense power of loving unconditionally that you are blessed with.

When you are able to accept this truth, you are also able to accept the choices of others without being judgmental. And this is just one evidence of unconditional love.

You must also understand that this is not a one-stop quick change. Slowly, taking one step at a time, you will be able to love yourself completely, and then you will be able to spread unconditional love or prema among people who surround you.

This is, in reality, the first step to enlightenment.

We all need healing. Almost all of us have something to release; we all have something to unblock. If we do not do it, it will be difficult for the soul to share unconditional love with people around it. The pathways of universal life-force energy or prana are generally blocked through diseases, fear, chronic pain, doubts, anxiety, spiritual troubles, and other negative energies.

Prema or unconditional love or Reiki can enable you to unblock these pathways and therefore lead to holistic happiness. Healing through Reiki or prema allows you to bring in elements of compassion in the healing process that lead to peace and balance the physical, emotional, mental, and spiritual side of the person. The channeling of energy into the body, aura, mind, and soul can enable you to experience loving and uplifting feelings, which in turn lead to a deep sense of inner harmony.

Where there is unconditional love, there is harmony. Where there is harmony, there is holistic happiness.

CHAPTER 7
Awakening the Kundalini Energy

* * *

THE ABILITY TO BALANCE YOUR life-force energy (or prana) between the ida and the pingala and the ability to allow this life-force energy to flow in the sushumna results in great joy and peace for the individual. This lays the foundation for "the awakening of the kundalini."

> Glory, glory to Mother Kundalini, who through Her Infinite Grace and Power, kindly leads the Sadhaka from Chakra to Chakra and illumines his intellect and makes him realize his identity with the Supreme Brahman. —Sri Swami Sivananda

I cannot stress the importance of awakening the kundalini energy. Irrespective of the spiritual or religious traditions that you may follow, it is important to understand that kundalini awakening is for all. It is the most important part of your spiritual realization or advancement.

A number of people read ancient Hindu scriptures or other books that talk about the union of *shiva* and *shakti* through kundalini awakening. The next step is that they want to experience this immediately. It is simply a natural desire. The most important part here is preparation. You need to prepare yourself to receive the immense amount of energy that will be released during the process.

To prepare for this process, ensure that your breath is balanced, your physical body is healthy, and your mind is stable. There are many methods to prepare yourself for this experience. Hatha yoga, raja-yoga, Kriya yoga, kundalini yoga, bhakti yoga, karma yoga, mantra chanting, and so on are some of them.

Whatever method you choose, it is very important to have some external guidance or guidance from your guru in order to ensure that you are preparing yourself well. A number of books and self-proclaimed teachers are available on this subject. These can, however, not be replaced by an authentic guru.

Your guru will not only guide you through your practice; he or she will also ensure that you develop the power to face any obstacle that comes in your way. The best part here is the advantage that you receive from the spiritual aura of your guru.

When the kundalini starts to awaken, the practitioner goes through experiences that can be counterintuitive. The ascension of kundalini is supposed to impart you energy, balance, wisdom, bliss, and realization. However, oftentimes you start experiencing pains and aches in the body, emotional instability, or a confused mental state during the ascension. Some of these unexpected experiences can be just your latent sanskaras working out, which is natural, while others could indicate that the methods that you are using to awaken your kundalini are incorrect and dangerous. Only a true guru who has gone this transformation himself or herself can distinguish between your experiences and guide you.

The proper ascension of kundalini requires the balancing of ida and pingala channels. An understanding of this process lays the foundation for raja-yoga.

The ancient Hindu scriptures describe kundalini as three different expressions.

- The first expression is the unmanifested cosmic energy. This is called *para-kundalini*.
- The second one is the *prana-kundalini* or the vital energy of the created universe.
- The third manifestation is consciousness or the *shakti-kundalini*; this is also called the intermediary between the other two.

Shakti-kundalini can be called the revealer of all mantras or your connections to the higher awareness. It is also called the eternal foundation of bliss flowing from sahasrara (crown chakra).

Shakti-kundalini evolves through a process called *shristi* karma (also called the process of creation). This involves descending from sahasrara through all the chakras. *Shakti-kundalini* sustains the physical body and its functions by remaining in the muladhara chakra. The muladhara acts like the plug point of the human body. Five of the remaining six chakras act like the plug. Through perseverance (*sthiti*) and practice, she ascends and awakens each chakra along the way.

The seventh chakra or the sahasrara acts as the lightbulb. As the power source plugs into the lightbulb, everything around it begins to glow. This is what happens when the kundalini is awakened. When the power source is properly plugged into the lightbulb, then keeping the lights on twenty-four seven will never be an issue. This must be done with absolute control and under the guidance of a spiritual guru.

As the kundalini ascends, the process of absorption of her *laya* karma ensures that she dissolves through the process of ascending and returning to sahasrara.

Shakti is termed *jagat mohini* (or world bewilder) as she descends to the lower chakras. In the process, she causes maya or delusion, ignorance, limitation, and obsession with material life. This process also ensures that she loses her subtlety and power.

The kundalini becomes subtler as she ascends through the chakras. She reabsorbs all the creativity that had initially descended from the sahasrara. This process is referred to as *laya* absorption. She eliminates the veils of maya, which evaporate like a mirage as she moves home. All mental limitations are removed, and consciousness shines through its original glory. Your mind becomes serene as all mental fluctuations settle down. This is now a vehicle for achieving that eternal happiness and bliss that we so much desire.

The kundalini merges with *shiva* at the sahasrara chakra. When present in formless state, she is consciousness. When present in creative form, she is *shakti*, which is also your power of manifestation.

Isn't it beautiful how the descent of kundalini elevates bondage, ignorance, and delusion? The ascending movement of the same kundalini energy leads to spiritual freedom and awakening.

If I were to explain *shiva* and *shakti*, I would say that they are similar to ink and the word. When you look at ink and the word, you look at two things:

- A static thing, which is the ink. It does not change. The composition of ink does not change, yet as it moves around, the same ink creates different words. This is the *shiva*. It is formless and does not change, and yet, it is responsible for the creation of the entire universe.
- The active aspect of the ink or the fluid, which moves around on the page to achieve different shapes. This is the *shakti*. It

can manifest itself as prana, chakra, kundalini, *panchmahabhutas* (the five elements), and so on.

The process of self-realization or the path to eternal happiness involves tracing the appearance of *shakti* (which appears to be "I") back to a point where *shiva* and *shakti* can be seen and experienced as one.

SIGNS OF KUNDALINI AWAKENING

The process of kundalini awakening is demonstrated through various signs and symptoms. These are of varying duration and intensity. Some of the commonly experienced signs are:

- involuntary shaking or jerkiness in the body
- feeling of cold in the body
- intense feelings of pleasure or bliss
- intense heat in a particular chakra or the spine
- a feeling of crawling snakes over hands and feet
- striking flows of energy, like electricity or internal lightning bolts
- spontaneous *mudras* (hand gestures), *asanas* (postures), *bandhas* (locks), or *pranayama* (breathing practices)
- a deep sense of uncertainty or confusion about what you are experiencing
- increase in the experience of inner colors and lights
- spontaneous or abrupt mood swings
- waves of intellectual, creative, or spiritual insights
- inner sounds, such as musical instruments, buzzing, roaring, or thunder

If you have prepared well for this experience with the help of your guru, then he or she will also be able to guide you so that you are ready to absorb this experience. This can be the beginning of your mental, physical, or emotional transformation. It is definitely one of the most important steps toward enlightenment.

CHAPTER 8
The Power of Unconditional Love or Reiki

✳ ✳ ✳

IF YOU ARE SOMEWHAT INTERESTED in spirituality or alternate healing, you must have heard about Reiki. A number of people mention that Reiki is energy or forms an important part of energy healing. According to me, Reiki is not an energy, It is true that from a traditional standpoint, Reiki means "life-force energy" or "spiritual energy." And that the word Reiki traces its origin to two words:

1. *Rei* implying "universal" and
2. *Ki* implying life force or life energy. This is the energy that constitutes everything in this universe

However, upon meditating on this at a much deeper level and connecting with Reiki, I realized that Reiki is actually beyond energy; it is a *para* energy. You may also call it the controller of all energies. As you go deeper, you find similarities between this concept and what the *Vedas* or yogic traditions refer to as *para shakti* and *param shakti*.

Let us first try to understand this.

Para shakti is the inherent nature of the Absolute; it is fully intelligent shakti, and it is not expressed in a certain way. People may say that you possess a certain nature, a typical nature. There are some innate tendencies that you possess that make you what you are and are responsible for this typical nature.

Para shakti is also called the *svarupa* shakti of the Absolute, where *svarupa* means "essential nature" or the "real form" of the Absolute. This means that para shakti is his own personal power.

Param shakti is the *prana* that circulates in this universe and our body as life force—and that is energy.

In order to be successful in this life and in this path, you must have access to both param and para shakti. In fact, if you have access to para shakti, you can reach a state of evolution where you can control the param shakti and generate energies as needed.

This also means that wherever you apply Reiki, either through touch healing or through distance healing (a process where using the power of thought, you are able to channel healing across time and space), the right type of energies will begin to accumulate. And that's the beauty of Reiki! It generates the right kind of healing energies as needed.

The nature of Reiki is harmony; wherever Reiki is applied, it creates a harmonious setting. This also implies that it restores balance. Reiki has its own infinite intelligence to address the root cause of any energy imbalance. Therefore, you can never go wrong with Reiki.

However, it is also important to understand that a lot of shakti-based *kriyas*, tantric mantras, or shakti-based mantras can lead to irreversible damage if applied in the wrong manner.

Reiki is represented by *Radha* in tales of Krishna or Mother Mary in the Bible.

The word *Radha* is composed of two syllables—*ra* and *dha*.

If you reverse these two syllables, it becomes *dha* and *ra*. Combine these together and you get the word *dhara*, which means "an outward flow." This outward flow is *aum* or the big bang out of which this universe was created.

As the dhara of aum flows outward, *Radha* keeps it in check. This signifies the presence of a centripetal force that is the outward force and a centrifugal force, which we call Reiki, that is the inward directing power that connects you to the Absolute. Once you get connected with this inward directing power, your journey toward the Absolute begins, simply because this is the natural nature of Reiki; Reiki naturally moves toward the Absolute.

The natural movement of param shakti or dhara or aum is movement away, because it is the sound of aum that was responsible for creating this creation.

Therefore, as soon as you get connected to Reiki, you get connected to *Radha*, and your journey back home begins. You begin your movement back to the Absolute.

The central theme of my teaching is that there are two fundamental powers in this universe and that we need both of these powers; one is the outward-flowing power or the power of aum, and the other is the inward-flowing power or the power of divine grace or *kripa*, which we refer to as *Reiki*. So aum is the centrifugal force flowing outward, and *kripa* is the centripetal force flowing inward, taking you toward the Absolute. These two powers are important to maintain the balance in this universe. If you look at your own life, there are times where you want to do more, and then, there are times when you feel content.

Life has always been a struggle between how much you should do and how much you should not do. Should you stop and enjoy what you already have, or should you make an effort to achieve the next big thing?

Spirituality or *yoga* is finding the balance between the two. In this path of Reiki raja-yoga, we connect you to the power of divine grace or *kripa* and the power of *aum*, the kundalini, or the willpower of the Divine. Through the process of consistent practice, we bring it to a point where this balance is achieved—where you know how much self-effort you need to make and how much you should surrender to the flow of this life.

And if you can master this art of the balance between self-effort and surrender, you can achieve optimum success. This means that you are able to achieve happiness and that you are not stressed or feeling that you are missing out on an opportunity, and at the same time, you are not becoming stagnant.

Ultimately, once this holistic happiness is achieved, you begin to penetrate this center of self-effort and surrender or *shiva* (which is surrender or the meditative state of stillness) and shakti (which is self-effort or the state of constant movement). The center of *shiva* and shakti is where *yoga* happens. The path of Reiki raja-yoga has the power to take you to this center by first establishing holistic happiness through the process of Reiki and *pranayama* and then through the process of deeper meditations and experiences of *samadhi*. Once this balance of centrifugal (or the outward) force and centripetal force (inward force) is achieved, a balance in life is also achieved.

Rei is often defined as "the higher intelligence that guides the creation and functioning of the universe." It is a subtle wisdom that infiltrates everything, animate as well as inanimate. This subtle wisdom controls the development of the entire universe—ranging from the development of life on this planet to the unfolding of galaxies in the universe. It is present to guide you whenever you need it.

Ki is defined as the inward-flowing force that takes you closer to the Absolute.

An important characteristic of ki is that it can respond to your feelings and thoughts. Ki flows with greater strength or is weakened depending on your feelings, emotions, and thoughts. Negative feelings and thoughts lead to a restricted ki.

In subsequent sections of this book, I will call this healing nature of Reiki Reiki power.

The secret to Reiki healing is that the practitioner transfers this healing power directly into the "healee," or the person being healed, by connecting him or her unswervingly to the supreme universal power. This power moves through the healer into the recipient.

If the healer is transferring his or her power into the recipient, wouldn't the healer experience a diminishing power?

Absolutely not!

This healing power is never depleted and is in fact utilized to heal and empower the healer. The healer is just a channel—a conduit. The source of the power is the Absolute. Another great thing about this power is that it goes where it is needed most. This implies that this power is an infinitely intelligent power. It can never be misused or abused and naturally directs itself in the direction it is required to flow in, implying that it does not require any deliberate direction by the healer. The healer performs his or her part by requesting Reiki to flow in a certain direction. However, this is a request only, which ultimately allows Reiki to heal those areas that require the most healing.

Along with the physical elements such as organs, organ systems, nerves, glands, arteries, muscles, bones, and so on, your body possesses a subtle energy system through which your vital life-force energy flows. This vital life-force energy comprises energy bodies that engulf your physical body and help you to process your emotions, thoughts, and ideas. We have already read about this in previous chapters.

Each energy body is linked to an energy center, which is referred to as a chakra. The chakras work like valves that enable this energy to pass through your spiritual, mental, physical, and emotional being. Your body also possesses energy meridians, which function like a river, carrying this energy through your body, nourishing it, and balancing your physical system, mental function, and spiritual purpose.

You are healthy and alive because of the presence of this life-force energy. A blockage in this energy leads to sickness and ill-health. Stress often weakens the flow of this energy and is also the leading cause of a number of lifestyle disorders.

Reiki channels new spiritual power into your energy bodies; this power has the nature of attracting the energies that are right for you and dissolving the energies that are stale or negative. This addresses the root cause of your weakened energy system. It reinstates the energy balance in your body and fills you with vigor and vitality by getting rid of the physical and emotional impact of this unreleased stress. It opens your blocked meridians and chakras very gently, yet powerfully. It clears your energy bodies and leaves you with a feeling of ultimate relaxation and peace.

According to the wisdom of Reiki and yogic sciences, disease is present in the seed form in our causal body. When it remains unchecked, it manifests as conscious or subconscious thoughts in our mental body. Gradually, it takes an emotional thought form and, then, an energy form.

From that point onward, if it is not checked, it takes a physical form, where it is manifested in the physical world and you can see and feel it. There are multiple opportunities to correct the disease. If you are able to remove all the seeds of disease from your causal body, then the manifestation into mental or emotional energies and physical bodies will not happen. Or if you are able to put a check on your thoughts, they will act as a filter and not let any thought of disease reach to the grosser layers of emotions and energy. The power of Reiki works on all of these layers at the same time.

It heals our causal body spiritually. The thoughts that you experience during your Reiki practice have the potential to heal your mental and emotional bodies, and of course, wherever this Reiki power is applied, it attracts and harmonizes all the needed energies at that particular point.

It is important to understand that this particular point does not have to be a point in the physical body; it could just be a concept or an event depending on your intention. The important thing is that whenever you apply Reiki power to this point, it has the potential to attract the right type and amount of energies for this point.

This energy can then heal the situation or, in this case, the point in the body. This further explains the versatility of Reiki where it addresses the full personality; not just the physical, mental, or emotional aspect but even the deeper recesses of your mind through regular practice are healed. This gift of Reiki is not available in any other healing technique.

Let us understand the process of energy depletion by imagining yourself as a new car, representing a young individual. This car is capable of charging its battery all by itself, simply by running around. And the battery remains in a perfectly healthy state irrespective of the weather conditions. However, as time passes, the process of aging sets in. The car starts experiencing damaged parts and is unable to hold its charge well. It runs well in summers or in less-demanding conditions. However, it demonstrates major breakdowns during demanding conditions such as the rainy or the winter season.

Your body experiences similar things. Just like the battery of the car, your body runs really well in your childhood, teenage, and early adulthood. The burden of responsibilities, family, job, mortgage, kids, and other relationships sets in the cycle of stress. And now, it needs charging!

This charge is provided through an external source via the Reiki power treatment. The battery charger is the power of divine grace or Reiki.

And without this divine grace, you experience powerlessness, helplessness, and ultimately, lifelessness!

In a nutshell, we can say that Reiki is the healing power of divine grace and the methodical way to channel it as unconditional love. This healing power is similar to what flows through Baba Ji Maharaj, Lord Krishna, Radha Ji, Jesus Christ, Mother Mary, and true saints and sages of all religions and spiritual paths.

Hence, Reiki essentially stands for the power of divine grace. It is also correct to refer to Reiki as the power of unconditional love. Grace is the unconditional love of the Divine toward you. In fact, I have found it easier to explain Reiki by referring to it as the power of unconditional love. It's just easier to understand it that way for most of you.

Unlimited unconditional love is the nature of the Divine and permeates the divine heart. It is also the essence or raw material of creation.

Therefore, the essence of our complete identity is unconditional love. This Love is also the *power to harmonize all energies*.

Hence, Reiki is the controller of all energies. It is *beyond energies*. In Sanskrit, it should therefore be called *para-oorja*.

Para = beyond, and *oorja* = energy.

Your ultimate goal is holistic happiness within yourself and in the world. The *way* to achieve this happiness is through *direct* connection to the divine heart and drawing *para-oorja* nourishment that can make you *healed*, *whole*, and *complete*.

BENEFITS THAT REIKI CAN OFFER

Here are some of the known benefits of Reiki:

- Reiki helps to balance and elevate your energy levels by clearing any blockages in the natural flow of energies in your body.
- It can be used to cleanse your body of the chemicals, poisons, and toxins present inside and around you.
- Reiki is also used as a preventive therapy to strengthen your body's energy field.
- It helps in diminishing stress.
- It enables you to experience relief from pain.
- It enables you to deal with depression, stress, and insomnia.
- Reiki induces a feeling of relaxation and is therefore used to relieve tension.

- It empowers you to connect with yourself at a subconscious level and provides valuable insight into the situations of your life.
- It accelerates the healing process.

Reiki engulfs you and comforts you just like warm and gentle sunshine, treating your body, mind, spirit, and emotions as whole. Extremely powerful, yet superbly relaxing, nourishing, and gentle, Reiki serves as an important complement to any other therapy.

You may want to tap into the unlimited supply of this life-giving power in order to elevate the quality of your life, enhance your health, or accelerate the healing process in your body, mind, and soul.

Reiki is known to demonstrate profound benefits, as this power works at all levels of your being and is therefore considered to be holistic, dealing with your physical, emotional, spiritual, and mental needs. It focuses on treating the root cause of the diseases rather than just the symptoms, therefore providing a long-term solution instead of a short-term fix.

A Typical Reiki Treatment

In order to receive Reiki treatment, you would be seated or lying down on a comfortable couch, accompanied with various kinds of guided meditations depending on your specific needs.

The healer will place his or her hands upon you with the intent to heal you. The power of unconditional love is then channelized from your healer into your body. This power normally travels through the healer's arms, into his or her hands, and then into the person receiving the Reiki treatment. It may, however, travel from any part of the healer's body into the recipient's body. The flow of this power is not directed by the healer. Though this power circulates throughout your body, it is most strongly felt where the healer's hands are placed.

HOW DOES A HEALER KNOW WHERE TO PLACE HIS OR HER HANDS?
Well, he or she relies on instinct and intuition.

Quite often, stagnant energy is eliminated and replaced by fresh clean energy during a Reiki session. And very often, this stagnant energy is present in an area different from the place of illness or injury. This is similar to a blocked inner tube of a bicycle. When air is unable to flow freely through this blocked inner tube, it causes a bulge in an area that bursts if it is filled with excess air. This results in permanent damage to the tube. A Reiki healer will not only unblock this blockage; he or she will also fix the puncture.

During a Reiki session, you would notice some warmth or heat emerging from your healer's hands. You may sometimes experience tingling in other areas of your body. You will feel extremely relaxed and may even fall asleep during a session. On awakening, you will be surprised by the magical feelings of relaxation and energy.

During a Reiki session, there is no effort from the healer to direct the energy to the recipient's body. This allows the energy to utilize its own intelligence and guide itself.

In order to transfer the healing power from your body to another person's body, you should be attuned to Reiki and demonstrate an intent to heal. This ensures a free flow of energy, with great benefits to the recipient.

Your body (physical and aura) has thirty-three focal points where various blocks get stored. Using Reiki, *para-oorja* can be directed to these thirty-three focal points through your hands and prayer to heal the blocks. Each point needs three minutes of healing. Before starting healing of the blocks, we undergo a process of "prayer," and after healing we give "thanks."

Reiki and the Psychosomatic Connection

The beauty of Reiki lies in the connection that it makes; there is a very traceable connection that it makes between our energy bodies, our spiritual bodies, and our physical bodies. I am yet to witness any other practice with such a deep and simple connection. This is a simple connection between your physical, mental, and emotional condition, as well as your aura.

As an example, Reiki believes that all physical symptoms that we experience through our body have a psychosomatic relationship with our mind and our emotions. This thought does coincide or comply with what Ayurveda says is the mother of all diseases. According to Ayurveda, the mother of all diseases is indigestion. When we think about indigestion, we tend to think about a physical indigestion or an upset stomach. Reiki has a different perspective on what indigestion means: indigestion is not just physical; it could be emotional or mental indigestion as well. Emotions that we are not able to suppress or express and thoughts that we are not able to assimilate or eliminate from our system lead to imbalances in our body. This leads to disease at the energy level, which then takes a pathological form in our body.

As we are talking about psychosomatic relationships and have discussed chakras already, I am reminded of a case that I was handling many years back where I met a very nice gentleman. He was very good at heart and very qualified but had a blocked solar chakra. He was going through a difficult time because whatever job he would take up, the company would shut down. He had worked with start-ups and yet did not find success. Then I took up the healing assignment and started focusing on his solar chakra; I started focusing on removing the blocks in his solar chakra. As I did that, his professional life changed completely, and he found tremendous success.

He was able to find a job where he was making the right amount of money and was happy in his role. In other words, he was finding the right kind of job contentment. Of course, it is an ongoing journey, where he continuously needs to work on his energy field to make sure that it is in top condition. Ultimately, this was a success story.

I thought I would mention this incident here in order to demonstrate to you how a block in your chakras can bring experiences that you may not like and how removing the blocks can alter the experience of life.

Let me take a step back and explain to you how Reiki power divides your body vertically into two halves. The right side of your body corresponds to your relationship with your own self and whoever you consider as near and dear to you. This could be your child or spouse or even somebody who is not related by blood to you but somebody you feel very closely about; you are mentally and emotionally connected to this person.

The left side of your body corresponds to your relationship with the other—whoever you consider as the world. Here again, it could be somebody who is a blood relative, but you may feel disconnected from him or her and feel that this relative is on the left side as the other.

In some cases the left side is also exhibited as accumulation of karma from your past life, and the right side is exhibited as the accumulation of karma in this life.

For example, in Reiki, shoulders have a psychosomatic sense of responsibility. This means that your right shoulder corresponds to your relationship with your own self—your sense of responsibility toward your own self and near and dear ones. If you feel that there is a lot of burden on your own self because of your family, because of the responsibilities that you have taken upon yourself—more burden than you can handle—then that thought, if not corrected, will lead to certain emotions and changes in your *pranic* energy field, and then this may create pain in your right shoulder.

Similarly, at work you could have a situation where, say, your boss is giving you a lot more work than you can handle and you feel that it is unfair; this thought will create emotions corresponding to the thought of just being too much or unable to bear. Gradually, these emotions will lead to changes in your energy field, which will create a physical pain in your left shoulder.

Your kidneys have a similar relationship: the right kidney has a relationship with your own self and near and dear ones, and the left kidney has a relationship with others. Now, consider that your relationship with your spouse is not good; there is a chance that you may develop kidney stones if that emotion of not getting along with your spouse is not checked for years and years. In this case, according to Reiki, this emotion will generate a stone in your right kidney.

Your lower back has your hurt feelings. A lot of times, I see people in my practice—people with chronic lower back pain—who go for massages and pain-relieving medications and ointments, but the pain keeps coming back. That is when we apply Reiki healing to the lower back—through touch healing or distance healing—and we teach them meditations to get rid of the hurt feelings that they might be suffering with or the suppressed feelings that they have. That is when the pain goes away and does not come back for a very long time. It is possible that it comes back because there may be a deep-rooted accumulation of energies of those feelings, but in most cases it just goes away because Reiki power starts healing those emotions and feelings. Of course, it also heals the physical aspect of the pain, and therefore a complete healing from the root cause happens.

So, this is a significant advantage that is demonstrated by Reiki power. The beauty of Reiki lies in eliminating the root cause of the disease, along with an amazing ability to connect the physical with the emotional, mental, and spiritual. It possesses the ability to connect what is abstract in a very simple way.

In a full body healing of the thirty-three points that I have described, you are not only healing the physical aspects of those points, but you are healing the psychosomatic relationships or conditions that those points correspond to.

Your liver and gallbladder area has the ability to process your emotions. If you are feeling that there are some pent-up emotions that you need to dissolve, as in when there are some unresolved emotions within your body, you could suffer from liver and gallbladder issues. These undissolved emotions get healed when you apply Reiki power to the liver and gallbladder area.

Your spleen and pancreas contain your suppressed anger that you have not been able to express for various reasons; these reasons could be constraints of the society that you live in, constraints of the job that you do, and so on. At the same time, when you are not able to digest that anger, it starts creating issues in the spleen and pancreas. People who are quick to anger have inflammation in the energy field around the spleen and pancreas. If not checked, this can lead to pancreatic cancer, and in those cases as well, Reiki becomes very important. When you heal the point near the spleen and pancreas, you are not only healing the physical aspects of spleen and pancreas but also sending spiritual healing to that inner anger that has no other avenue to vent out—and that is the beauty of Reiki!

Your knees have fears—the right knee having fear regarding yourself—inner fear that you are not able to express. Your left knee has fears regarding the outside world.

During our Reiki raja-yoga seminars, I go into detail of what these points are and guide the attendees to be able to heal these points in the right order to be able to not only heal the physical aspects of the body but to be able to influence the *pranic*, the emotional and mental aspects too.

Once all the blocks in our emotional and mental energy field are removed, we achieve holistic happiness and self-realization because these blocks were preventing a full unfoldment of our personality. These blocks were preventing us from understanding our true self and preventing our self-realization.

Of course, one should never give medical diagnosis based on what the Reiki belief system says because Reiki healers are not doctors and you should never stop your regular medical treatment. These are just guiding posts that can help you, but you have to introspect on them and then make a decision based on your condition as to how you want to use the power of Reiki raja-yoga to physically and spiritually heal yourself.

A Brief History of Reiki

There are many versions available regarding the history and origin of Reiki. One of the most prevalent versions is provided here.

Mikao Usui was born in Taniai village in Yamagata county, Gifu Prefecture of Japan, on 15th August 1865. Mikao's family was wealthy and belonged to the Tendai sect of Buddhism. In order to receive primary education, Mikao was sent to a Tendai Monastery at the age of four, where he was also taught martial arts. (He learned Kiko—a martial art discipline focused on elevating your health—use of chi, and some healing techniques, including healing with hands.) He started practicing meditation, which enabled him to strengthen his ability to boost his personal chi. (This knowledge was put to good use later in his career.) It is believed that Usui traveled to America and Europe for studies. He learned theology, philosophy, and medicine, and also graduated with a doctorate in Japanese literature.

Mikao Usui married Sadako Suzuki and resided in Kyoto with their two children (a boy named Fuji and a girl named Toshiko). He studied the Buddhist way of healing and also invested his time in psychic practices such as Shintoism and Shugendo. He wished to benefit mankind by understanding and passing on the methods of healing to future generations. Most of his money and time was spent in studying and understanding the Buddhist healing techniques and symbols.

A metaphysical group named Rei Jyutsu Kai included Mikao Usui as one of its members. This was due to the commendable psychic ability Mikao possessed. The base location of this group was the holy mountain called Kurama Yama, and it is believed that a ritual named distant healing was practiced by members of this group. Usui became inquisitive about distant healing but he found out from one of his students that the treatment was not really effective and did not last long. During this time, hands-on healing was also practiced in Japan. It is said that during this process, the healers were transferring their own chi energy to the recipients, making them unwell.

Usui believed that there could be a better mechanism to heal and intensified his quest for satori or spiritual enlightenment. He wanted to understand the deeper meanings of certain symbols in order to serve mankind better. Usui decided to fast on Mount Kurama for twenty-one days and seek divine guidance. He sat on the ground and under a waterfall, placed twenty-one stones before him, and let the stream of water fall on his head while he practiced meditation. This kind of meditation opens and purifies the crown chakra. He would remove one stone at the end of each day in order to count the number of days. On removing the last stone, he experienced bright light approaching him with a lightning-fast speed. This made him lose consciousness and filled him with the light of knowledge, understanding of Reiki healing, and the gift of his own attunement. He suddenly understood the meaning of all the symbols (called Reiki symbols today).

Usui was overjoyed about his achievement and rushed down the mountain, only to realize that he had stubbed his toe and injured his foot badly. He decided to heal his foot with Reiki and experienced the first miracle—his foot stopped bleeding, and the pain vanished. He realized that apart from the illuminating experience that he had achieved, he had also achieved the gift of healing.

Usui opened a center in Aoyama, Harajuku, Tokyo in April 1922, and began teaching people and offering healing sessions. Usui's fame spread, and he became well-known as a healer and a teacher. People traveled great distances to receive his guidance and healing. Usui's system became very popular with the armed forces, and particularly the Imperial Navy, because they were looking for traditional ways of healing that did not require large stocks of medical equipment and drugs to be carried on board the ships. Around 1925, he was visited by a group of naval officers. Among the officers was Chujiro Hayashi, who became a master student of Usui and continued the lineage after Usui's passing away.

Usui passed away on March 9, 1926, due to a stroke and left the world with the five principles of Reiki and the three pillars of Reiki. According to his memorial, Usui taught over two thousand people to practice his Reiki techniques, and trained twenty teachers.

Mikao Usui is considered the first *sensei* or master of Reiki. I am the ninth *sensei* in the lineage of Mikao Usui.

MENTION OF REIKI IN THE ANCIENT INDIAN TEXTS

1. Gods, raise again the man whom ye, O Gods, have humbled and brought low.
   Ye Gods, restore to life again, him, Gods! who hath committed sin.
2. Here these two winds are blowing far as Sindhu from a distant land.
   May one breathe energy to thee, the other blow thy fault away.
3. Hither, O Wind, blow healing balm, blow every fault away, thou Wind!
   For thou who hast all medicine comest as envoy of the Gods.
4. May the Gods keep and save this man, the Maruts' host deliver him.
   All things that be deliver him that he be freed from his offence.
5. I am come nigh to thee with balms to give thee rest and keep thee safe.
   I bring thee mighty strength, I drive thy wasting malady away.
6. Felicitous is this my hand, yet more felicitous is this.
   This hand contains all healing balms, and this makes whole with gentle touch.
7. The tongue that leads the voice precedes. Then with our tenfold-branching hands.
   With these two healers of disease, we stroke thee with a soft caress. —*Atharva Veda*, book 4, hymn 13

The concept of "makes whole" is a tradition that still continues in Reiki healing affirmations. "The tongue that leads the voice precedes" refers to the chants that were used in ancient times while healing. These chants were rediscovered by my guru, late Shri Vijay Bansal, through his direct realization. The "tenfold-branching hands," of course, refers to the ten fingers.

The first mention of Reiki in the *Atharva Veda* was pointed out by Dr. Nalin Narula in his book *Joy of Reiki*. Dr. Nalin Narula was the initiating master of my guru. Shri Vijay Bansal added raja-yoga techniques to Reiki and made this spiritual system the most powerful system available to the masses.

For those who can read Devnagari script, below is the excerpt from the *Atharva Veda*:

अयं मे हस्तो भगवानयं मे भगवत्तरः ।
अयं मे विश्वभेषजोऽयं शिवाभिमर्शनः ॥६॥

हस्ताभ्यां दशशाखाभ्यां जिह्वा वाचः पुरोगवी ।
अनामयित्नुभ्यां हस्ताभ्यां ताभ्यां त्वाभि मृशामसि ॥७॥

THE PRINCIPLES OF REIKI
Here are the five principles of Reiki that have their roots in the teachings of Usui Sensei:

- Just for today: I will live in the attitude of gratitude.
- Just for today: I will not fear or worry.
- Just for today: I will not be angry.
- Just for today: I will be honest to my own self.
- Just for today: I will respect all living beings.

My guru, Shri Vijay Bansal, added another principle:

- Just for today: I will not let my ego-personality judge myself.

The essence of Reiki is explained below.

Just for today: The importance of "today" is highlighted in all six principles. Today defines your present. It teaches you to live each and every moment of the day completely; life just becomes a collection of moments. It is easier to make a commitment to these principles for one day at a time rather than making a lofty commitment to follow these throughout your life to come. You will find more success when you affirm and commit to these principles on a daily basis.

I will live in the attitude of gratitude: Reiki encourages you to be thankful, receiving and giving the gift of the universe. You should be thankful about everything in your life—the good, the bad, and the ugly. Being thankful breaks the cycle of misery. If you are going through a bad time or suffering, then it is because of some karma that was performed in the past, which has become the cause of suffering today. If you start brooding over this and blaming others, you just sink deeper into that misery. By being thankful for whatever you have and whatever situation you are in, you break the cycle of misery; you break the influence of that effect on you, and gradually that thought process leads you out of the suffering that you are in. It creates a new cause for good things to happen in your life.

I will not fear or worry: The principles of Reiki encourage you to trust the universe completely. They tell you to let go of your fears and worries, make the best possible efforts, and leave the rest in the hands of the universe. This frees you from your fears, and you start believing in the universe.

Fear begets more fear; worry begets more worry. The moment you stop worrying, you demonstrate your faith in the Absolute, and the moment that demonstration happens, the powers of Reiki (the para shakti) and the powers of prana and aum (the param shakti) descend on you and begin to support you. So, don't let fear create more fear and don't let worry create more worry. Just for today, live without fear or worry.

I will not be angry: This principle encourages you to stay away from anger and attain perfect balance of emotion and mind through Reiki. It guides you to live a peaceful and calm life.

Anger burns your positive karma and reduces the power of your soul. In some cases, you can be angry about rightful causes. I believe in positive anger as well. However, it has to be channeled correctly. And in all circumstances, it is better to not be angry and think about the situation in a positive manner. This does not mean that you become inert and do not respond to a situation; it simply means that you act with equanimity and understand the situation that you are in. That is the best way to not burn your positive karma and use it to your advantage.

I will be honest to my own self: Reiki shows you how to integrate and utilize the power of honesty for everyday work. It reiterates the importance of work and how working honestly can enable you to lead a meaningful life, growing and learning every day.

Honesty toward your own self is extremely important. When you are honest to your own self, you increase the power of your soul and let it work through your mind and body. Honesty toward your own self aligns your soul, mind, and body. When you are not honest with your own self, you disintegrate. Your chakras start to fall out of alignment, and you are not able to draw the right amount of power from your soul into your mind. This dishonesty to your own self weakens your mind and the power of your soul. Yoga is about alignment and integration of all the chakras, and the first step to do this is to be honest to your own self.

I will respect all living beings: This principle started out as ***"I will be respectful of my parents and elders"***. Over a period of time, this has been expanded into "Just for today, I will respect all living beings." Whatever learning you have achieved is because of your parents and elders, and also people around you. When you interact with people, you learn some things, and you share some good experiences and some bad experiences; you need to respect people for all that they are teaching you. This respect also empowers you to see everybody as your own extended self. This does not mean that you should not be cautious and that you should not apply your judgment when interacting with people; it just means that you act with respect under all circumstances and that you are never hateful or spiteful.

Reiki encourages you to nurture a sense of oneness and love. It mentions that there is one single soul in this universe and this soul does not distinguish between self and others. Therefore, when you are kind to others, you are kind to yourself!

I will not let my ego-personality judge myself: You are constantly judging yourself; you criticize yourself for your follies and praise yourself for the numerous achievements that you make. The criticism specifically weakens or blocks your mind. When you stop judging yourself, you also empower yourself to not judge others. Life is not about judging yourself or judging people around you; it is all about living.

Therefore, Reiki encourages you to not belittle yourself or anyone else. You must not run yourself down in your own eyes or in anyone else's eyes. At the same time, you must also not over elevate yourself. Reiki encourages you to be humble; that way you get free from the clutches of your ego.

Meditating on these principles every single day allows you to live life in a richer way.

The Three Pillars of Reiki

Usui Sensei has provided information about the three pillars of using Reiki:

- Your body is your **temple of the spirit**, and it is your responsibility to treat it with respect and care for it. Usui himself practiced Kiko (a system of cultivating and mastering energy) in order to gain strength and suppleness and refill his own energies. Practicing yoga can help you maintain perfect health and wellness too. You can also receive Reiki from others at frequent intervals.
- You are also encouraged to **look after your mind**. Usui looked after his mind by meditating every day. Meditation should be a part of your lifestyle too, especially due to the demands laid out by the stressful lifestyle of today.
- You should **focus on caring for society** by giving Reiki to others. Always remember that Reiki flows through you. Therefore, the more you care for others and treat others through Reiki, the more you benefit.

The Three Laws of Reiki

In addition to the principles and the pillars of Reiki, an understanding of the three laws of Reiki will give you guidance and a sense of relief, no matter how difficult a situation you are in.

The first law is **Like attracts like**. This law states that your circumstances become whatever you are or however you think. So, if you think positive, then positive things happen in your life. If you think negative from inside, then you begin to attract negative things in life.

The second law states that **Energy follows thought**. This means that the power of Reiki and all associated energies that Reiki attracts move in the direction of your thoughts. So, if you are thinking about finding a new job, Reiki will begin to flow in that direction, and all the energies needed to get you that new job start accumulating in the direction of your desire. Similarly, if you focus on a certain part in your body, Reiki and all the associated energies will start flowing there. In the yogic texts, there is a teaching that states *"Jahan Chitta, Vahan Prana."* Here, Chitta means attention, and prana means that life-force energy. According to the statement, your prana will move wherever your chitta is.

Therefore, this teaching is validated from Reiki as well as the yogic viewpoint. This also means that if you have to move your prana somewhere, you just have to focus your energies at that point and prana moves there. My understanding, based on my meditation, is that whenever we are thinking about something for more than three minutes, we start giving birth to that idea. It does not mean that that idea manifests itself in the physical world. However, its birthing process begins in those three minutes—good or bad. So, if you are worried about your child not returning home on time safely and you are continuously worried about it, then gradually you are giving birth to that idea of your child not returning home safely. I am not saying that you become completely reckless and carefree and not pay attention to the practical things in life, but you do have to be mindful of your thoughts and make sure that they do not become too negative. It is all right to be practical, alert, and intelligent and exercise caution, but you must remember that the pendulum should not swing too much toward negativity, because if you are thinking about something in a really negative manner, you are giving a practical birth to that imagination. That is precisely the idea behind energy follows thought.

The third law of Reiki is that **All disease is due to lack of Reiki, and everything and anything can be healed given sufficient Reiki**. This is a very important and relieving law to hear about. It is important to understand that all disease in the body, mind, emotions, and aura is because of lack of love.

People get addicted to alcohol, smoking, and other addictions. You ask them probing questions, and you discover that there was some lack of love in their life that drove them toward an unhealthy addiction. Reiki is nothing but unconditional love, and you have seen that in the previous chapters.

Now, consider this: you are applying love to a disease that is caused due to lack of love.

In due course of time, this love that you are applying will ensure that the disease gets cured. This does not imply that you should stop external scientific medical treatments. I always insist that you should not stop medical treatment but should use Reiki as a complementary therapy and experience where it takes you.

A Mantra to Meditate Upon

Given that the rediscovery of Reiki happened in Japan and Usui Sensei had Buddhist roots, the gurus that I learned Reiki from held the following mantra in high esteem:

"Nam myoho renge kyoho"

A simple explanation of this mantra is that "I fully believe in the universal karmic law of the Divine."

This Buddhist mantra, written in the Japanese language, can transform your life when you regularly chant or meditate upon it.

Nam: is derived from the Sanskrit word *namu*, which means "to devote oneself." *Namu* means action and attitude. Therefore, through this mantra, you are initiated into correcting the actions that you need to take and developing the attitude that is required to attain oneness with the Absolute.

Myoho: *Myoho* refers to the mysterious principles that govern the working of the universe every single minute. It also implies that you are blessed with the qualities that you need to develop into your life.

Renge: *Renge* implies the lotus flower, which blooms in a muddy pond and still retains its pristine nature. This signifies that any ordinary person can achieve oneness with the Absolute even in the midst of day-to-day struggles.

Kyoho: *Kyoho* implies sound or rhythm. It means that everything in the universe is a manifestation of the mystic law.

The Attunement Process

Reiki is not taught in a traditional college scenario. It is transmitted from the Reiki master into the student during the process of attunement. This process opens the chakras in your body and establishes an exceptional connection between the Reiki source and the student.

The Reiki attunement is an extremely impactful spiritual experience that involves channelization of spiritual power into the student through the medium of a Reiki master. It helps to connect the student to the Reiki power source. This process is monitored by the *Rei* or God-consciousness, which helps in making adjustments in the process based on the specific requirements of each student. Various Reiki guides and spiritual gurus are present during the process of attunement, and they enable the student to implement the process. You may experience some personal messages, past life experiences, specific healings, sound and vision, or any other kind of mystical experiences during or after this process.

The process of attunement may elevate your psychic sensitivity, and you may experience increased intuitive awareness, opening of the third eye, or any other psychic ability after receiving a Reiki attunement.

Having received Reiki attunement means that Reiki stays with you throughout your life. Of course, you need to practice regularly to keep Reiki flowing effectively in your energy bodies and in your life. You typically require one attunement to reach a particular level; however, additional attunements may bring greater benefits, including refinement of the Reiki energy you are channeling, an elevated strength of energy, clarity of mind, healing of personal problems, enhanced level of consciousness, and an elevated psychic sensitivity.

The process of Reiki attunement initiates a cleansing process that impacts your emotions, body, and mind. It empowers you to release the stored toxins and harmful chemicals from your body and initiates a process of purification. In fact, a specific process of purification is recommended prior to an attunement process. This enhances the results of your attunement process.

The attunement process in the Indian tradition is named *diksha*, which is a Sanskrit word. The word *diksha* is composed of two words—*da* (pronounced the), which means to give, and *kshi*, which means to destroy. *Diksha* means "from the guru to the initiate"—giving of the spiritual power that leads to the destruction of darkness or ignorance present in the initiate, knowingly or unknowingly.'

So, the process of attunement can simply be referred to as the transfer of spiritual power from guru to the initiate.

Another meaning is derived from the verb root *diksh*, which means to consecrate. The consecration or making holy of your energy bodies is an important part of the transformation that happens during the diksha process.

It can be said that dikhsa begins where the teachings that you acquire from reading through the Internet and books stop and transformation begins.

This transformation cannot happen through reading; it happens within yourself, and the intervention of the guru as a channel of the spiritual power of Reiki acts as a transforming agent for you.

There is another important thing that happens during the process of attunement: all the knowledge that the guru has been graced with and the guru's guru or the param gurus that came before your guru—all of their knowledge is condensed in the seed form, and that gives you a boost in your spiritual progress and helps you progress in life too. All this education that has taken more than thousands of years to acquire is transferred to you in a very short time frame, and then it is upon you to convert that potential knowledge that has been transferred to you into something that you can understand and make use of through regular practice. This boost accelerates your spiritual evolution sometimes by hundreds of years; this attunement has to be considered very respectfully, and it is a privilege to be able to get initiated by a true guru into a spiritual practice.

WHAT HAPPENS POST THE ATTUNEMENT PROCESS?

- The process of attunement places you at par to the group of people who utilize the power of Reiki to heal themselves, one another, and the environment.
- Reiki is not a religion but can empower you to practice your religion in a better manner, along with enabling you to experience greater spiritual energy and enlightenment.
- Your chakras open up, and you are able to connect to the divine Reiki source.

- You become aware of what is expected out of you when it comes to healing yourself or others.
- You convert into a more psychic and intuitive individual.
- The overall quality of your life improves!

THE LEVELS IN REIKI

The path of Reiki raja-yoga integrates Reiki and raja-yoga and comprises seven levels.

The traditional Reiki system has three and sometimes even four levels. In Reiki raja-yoga, because it is a much deeper practice and takes you into deeper levels of realization, we have seven levels. There could be levels beyond level seven because the Absolute is infinite and you can keep expanding in the Absolute; there is no beginning and no end to the Absolute.

In traditional Reiki, level one is called *shodan*, level two is called *okuden*, and level three is called *shinipidan*. Typically in level three, according to the traditional approach, you are made a master of Reiki.

I have differed from that approach. I do not create masters at level three because for me a master who can initiate others must have a deeper understanding of the self; he or she has to have a stature of at least a *swami*—self-master—or a *guru*, which stands for somebody who takes you from *gu* (darkness) to *ru* (light). So, as you progress through the levels, you move from darkness to light. However, in order to be a master and light the light of enlightenment and healing into others, you must have achieved your own enlightenment to a great degree. Hence, I am a little stricter than the traditional approach.

Nowadays you can get mastership in Reiki online without any initiation process or practice. That is simply commercialization of Reiki, which I am completely against. This trivializing of the spiritual powers of the East is what diminishes these techniques and creates misconceptions about Reiki, Kriya yoga, and raja-yoga.

Coming back to the levels in Reiki raja-yoga...we have seven levels.

Before we attempt to understand these levels, let us first look at the spiritual construction of this universe. There are three planes of consciousness—*aum*, *tat*, and *sat*.

Aum, tat, and sat form the three spheres of this construction. Aum is the electromagnetic zone, so the manifested world that we see around us—the trees, mountains, water, anything that is visible and created out of solidification of energies—is aum.

Anything that is invisible but in energy form, like heat, wind, and so on, are all in aum. There are 1,089 planes of existence within aum itself.

At **level one**, our aim is to connect the initiate who might be at level two or three in the plane of aum upward toward the seven hundredth plane of aum. We aim for the 752nd plane, but anything above 700 is considered as good, depending on the deservingness of the initiate.

In the traditional Usui Healing System in Reiki Level I, you understand and learn the hand positions that you can use to perform Reiki on yourself or on anybody else. You also develop an understanding of the Reiki principles and the history of Reiki before receiving your attunement. The process of attunement makes you a Reiki practitioner, and practicing Reiki remains your choice.

Reiki level one initiates a process of self-healing and self-discovery. Your knowledge of Reiki can bring better insight into the functioning of your soul. It also helps you to connect with your mental, physical, spiritual, and emotional self, which empowers you to understand self and others. Quite often, the places that you feel are "no-problem" areas require maximum attention.

In **level two**, our aim is to connect the initiate to the juncture of aum and tat; we connect initiates to the plane 1,089 and above, and they go into tat, which is the plane of universal intelligence. It is a purely magnetic plane of consciousness comprised of intelligences that are responsible for the running of this universe. It is the plane where the higher heavens exist. Aum is the plane where all the astral heavens exist, whereas tat is the plane where higher intelligent heavens exist.

According to the traditional system, level two includes emotional healing, distant healing, and mental healing, along with an understanding of the three Reiki symbols (harmony, focus, and connection). Developing this understanding enables you to achieve the next level of attunement and elevates your power of healing.

The path of Reiki raja-yoga taught at the Divine Heart Center encourages the use of empowered Sanskrit mantras revealed directly to our gurus. These mantras are more powerful than the traditional Reiki symbols in enhancing the flow of Reiki. Each mantra captures the essence of the symbol but creates a stronger healing light and vibration than the symbols.

In **level three**, our aim is to connect the initiate to a much higher plane at the juncture of tat and sat. Sat is the plane of pure consciousness and bliss. The juncture of tat and sat is also called the son of God area. Without going too much into esoteric spirituality, I just want to remind you that this is a very high plane, where you are connected to the most stable point in the universe; you are connected to a place where the sons of Gods descend from. This is the plane where Jesus Christ descended from. One of the highest forms of Lord Vishnu resides at the juncture of tat and sat.

Traditionally, teachings at level three include a thorough understanding of the Usui master symbol and its meaning, along with its application. The Usui master symbol completes the other three symbols, which are taught at level two.

Level four upward is a different journey altogether; it cannot be explained in words. Level four and up are given to the most serious initiates who want to make Reiki raja-yoga their lifestyle and ultimate goal in life or their *paramarth* (*param* means ultimate, and *arth* means goal or meaning); when self-realization becomes your ultimate meaning in life, that means you are initiated into level four and up. In level four our goal is to connect you to the plane of sat—pure consciousness or pure essence of this creation, God himself. This level connects to the highest manifestation of the Lord as the Creator or *Ishvar*.

Levels five, six, and seven are initiations that cannot be quantified or expressed in words. They are all in the plane of sat, and some of them are beyond it. I have made Reiki raja-yoga masters after they have completed many years of spiritual practice and gone through spiritual transformation themselves. Then they have been connected to higher planes of sat, and that is where they draw their power from.

So, aum, tat, and sat are the three broad levels of connection. They are equivalent to the Holy Spirit, which is aum; the Son, which is tat; and the Father, which is sat.

This is where we have taken the practice of Reiki raja-yoga; **we have made it much deeper than the traditional Reiki by combining the deeper elements of raja-yoga, specifically Kriya yoga, and ultimately through the seven levels, we guide the initiate into the**

state of samadhi, where *sam* means "at par with" and *adhi* means "the object of highest attention."

As you progress through these seven levels, you reach the state of *samadhi* or absolute absorption in the *Divine*. A lot of times, if you are just looking at fulfilling your material needs or to resolve a specific issue (it could be health, job, career, or some mental relief and stress reduction), up to level three is more than sufficient for you.

This is the power that this practice provides.

In fact, level two is also great for people who are looking at living a happy life. From level three upward, a transformation happens where your goal changes from just wanting holistic happiness to wanting self-realization. And unless that shift in your inner core desire has happened, there is no point getting initiations higher than level three.

I have been very selective about giving higher initiations in order to maintain the quality, depth, and power of this practice.

Another important thing to be understood about initiation is that all of us are exposed to Reiki. The power of Reiki is present everywhere; it permeates this universe. But not all of us are tuned to this power. In a similar way as on a television you can watch the news channel, the cartoon channel, the sitcoms, or the wild life—whatever you desire to watch; however, you have to tune the television by way of the remote control or the button and adjust the frequencies to receive the transmission of a particular channel.

Similarly, people who are uninitiated into any spiritual discipline are not properly tuned to the power of Reiki. When you were born as a child, you were naturally tuned to the power of Reiki. However, this tuning diminished as you let your ego take you over and your past karma then began to manifest. This tuning or connection between the universal power of Reiki and your chakras is called *antahkarana*. This *antahkarana* is the pillar of consciousness that connects ourselves to the power of Reiki.

In a person who is not initiated into any spiritual discipline, this *antahkarana* is very, very narrow; it is a pillar, almost like a tube of light, that passes from the crown chakra into the lower chakras and is very small—just like the tip of a pencil. Through the attunement process, this *antahkarana* is widened. I have seen the *antahkarana* widen from the tip of a pencil to about half an inch in diameter to one inch in diameter. Without an attunement, such a rapid transformation in the size of the *antahkarana* and in turn the flow of the Reiki power from the universe into your body is not possible.

It can take hundreds of years of spiritual effort on your own to create changes in the size of the *antahkarana* that is receiving the Reiki power from the universe into your body. Whereas in the initiation process, through the secret techniques that the gurus are taught from their gurus and ultimately from the Absolute through a process of self-realization, these techniques expand the *antahkarana*, and there is brought about a quantum leap in the consciousness, where you are able to draw more Reiki power from the universe into your body. Such progress is not possible by any means other than proper attunement by an authentic guru of Reiki raja-yoga or any other true spiritual discipline.

When the practitioner is new to Reiki, in level one seminars we teach them touch healing. They sometimes experience Reiki as a tingling sensation throughout their body or wherever they keep their hands as a part of full-body touch healing. They may also experience heat sensation or cold sensation, and that is their first experience of Reiki—typically—because once the Reiki power starts entering their energy systems, it generates energy to cut through the negative energy that is already there.

And when this happens, heat is generated due to the drilling effect of the negative energy. But when the negative energy leaves the body, the practitioner feels a cooling sensation, and by this process, the practitioner develops some faith in the power of Reiki; even though this may not be complete faith, there is faith that yes, something is happening.

As you advance into Reiki and move into higher initiations, you experience Reiki as a force; this force is different from energy. Energy has feelings of vibration, heat, or cold. But force feels like an attraction or repulsion—almost like an emotional love, where if you are very attracted toward somebody, you feel a force in your heart that attracts you toward him or her, or if you dislike somebody, you feel a repulsion.

As you go deeper into Reiki or when Reiki reveals its deeper self to you, you are attracted toward the *satvik* qualities in life (these are essentially the positive qualities in life). There may be repulsion toward the negative things in life (such as alcohol or other addictions, and you naturally feel like going away from them). This relationship with Reiki develops almost like *Radha* and Krishna or mother and child, where you feel attracted toward love and grace, and in the process, you yourself become loving and caring.

As you progress even deeper, then Reiki in the final stages reveals itself as a power, and you begin to experience Reiki as being present everywhere you go. It is just a presence; it is not a tingling sensation—whereas in some cases it might be because the energy system is constantly balancing itself. Even if you become an advanced *yogi* (or an advanced healer), you may sometimes feel it as a pull or push. The height of your experience at the later stages would be experiencing Reiki in its true nature—which is always there—as the power of divine grace, constantly assuring you, healing you, and healing those around you.

At this time, the healer's presence starts becoming a healing technique in itself.

So, if a very advanced healer is sitting in a bus, everybody around him or her will get healed based on their receptivity. The advanced healer realizes Reiki as the power that is present everywhere, and this realization also endows upon the healer the power of the **healing presence**. This power of healing presence is the ultimate stage in a Reiki practitioner's journey.

This is the unfoldment of Reiki—*from energy to a force to a power.*

It is imperative to execute self-treatment once a day for twenty-one days post receiving any level of attunement. This process enables you to heal yourself.

You also get the empowerment to heal others once you are attuned to Reiki power. Practicing on your own self gets the Reiki power flowing and initiates the process of healthy healing. It must be noted that Reiki is not an alternative to traditional medical practice, but an extremely impactful complementary therapy.

It is advisable to meditate every day post receiving the attunement to level one. Meditation elevates your power to heal yourself and heal others.

Reiki—Crystals, Intentions, and Clothing

A number of crystals and *yantras* are used during the practice of Reiki. These help in accelerating the healing process. Most of these are programmed with spiritual power that provides protection to the wearer. Intention-healing cards, clothing with special prints, aura-healing crystals, and meditation music are available at the Divine Heart Center.

These are charged with spiritual power from the guru and can also be customized to heal a particular situation.

Quite often, when you visit new age markets or if you have had a chance to visit India, you see a lot of crystals of different shapes (pyramids or other shapes) being sold. Crystals do emit healing energies, but one has to be careful in buying crystals because the energies that the crystals emit need to be in tune or favorable to your own energy field. They should not conflict with your own energy field; otherwise, the purpose of the crystal is diminished. In fact, in many cases, especially in the cases of gemstones, which are crystals of higher quality, crystals can have harmful as well as beneficial effects on your aura and in turn your life when not chosen correctly.

When you purchase a crystal from a market, it is like a blank CD; it is empty and does not have any music or data on it. It may have some data as a result of the process of mining or transportation. During this process, the energy that it was exposed to gets stored in the crystal. Therefore, simply picking up a crystal from the market and keeping it inside your home is never a useful thing. The energies could be positive, but they are not enhanced so as to make some significant progress in your life.

As part of the Reiki raja-yoga practice, a lot of trained healers program the crystals. As I mentioned, the crystals are like blank CDs; however, they have the quality of being able to store information in the form of healing energies, and a guru or a trained healer can program the crystals. There is a specific way in which you program the crystals, and that is what puts the music onto the CD. The actual benefit of the crystal is realized only after it is programmed to its maximum potency in order to provide you the maximum benefit. Therefore, you should always buy crystals that are blessed or programmed by a true guru or healer so that you are able to achieve maximum benefit by using them. This guru or healer will also be able to guide you on what crystals to wear.

Typically in my healing practices, I use natural quartz. It is a very clean crystal that can be used by anyone; it promotes peace. When effectively programmed, crystals can also improve the aura of a house, office, and so on. The size does not matter much. Of course, a larger-size crystal will have a bigger energy field. However, the quality and programming of the crystal matters a lot, so even a small good-quality crystal, if it is programmed properly, will completely change the energy and aura of your home.

I often refer to crystals as frozen flames. Many times people light up candles in front of their altars or light *diyas* or lamps of clarified butter, ghee, or oil to generate positive energy or to dispel negative energy. Crystals are like frozen flames because they also emit energies; they are a safer alternative to the candles and do not involve any risk of fire. You can keep them in your altar. You must remember to clean them regularly.

Keeping your crystals respectfully and cleaning them regularly can provide you the benefits of an oil lamp twenty-four seven, and that's a secret about crystals that makes me refer to them as frozen flames.

A Reminder about Spiritual Basics

Various people in the world view spirituality in various ways. Some people believe in the presence of God, and there are others who have an issue with the very existence of God. You are definitely not a nonbeliever, and I say this with conviction because you picked up this book.

Christians, Jews, Muslims, Hindus—all worship an omnipotent God. The Buddhists and the Taoists view God as an Absolute state of consciousness. David Goddard, in his book *Tree of Sapphires*, mentions:

> There are potential drawbacks to thinking of the Supreme Reality as either a person or a state. Because all images are concepts based on finite experience…In conceiving the Absolute as a person, you embrace the idea, in your subconscious, that some things may be given or withheld by that person—that some beings are favored and others not. On the other hand, when you conceive of the One Reality as a state, you imply that there is no personal relationship and that you must reach it unaided by the ineffable, solely by your own efforts.

Why am I bringing this up here? Well, this is because I want you to align yourself with the divine principles, the Absolute, the God, or the universal consciousness—however you may want to express this.

You can be sure about your life leading you in the right direction through meditation, prayer, intent to heal, and alignment with the Absolute, God, or universal consciousness. We have talked about this in the previous chapters. Here is a short recap:

Your higher self or spirit: You are a part of your higher self, your spirit, or your consciousness, which constitutes a greater part of you. Only a small portion of this spirit is incarnated as your soul. Your higher self is too great a consciousness to fit into your soul. This higher self is guided by a greater consciousness to grow and learn, and does not experience the fear or pain that your ego covering your soul may experience. As somebody striving to learn Reiki, you should accept that you are a part of this universal consciousness and try to align yourself to it. This will enable you to become happy and healthy and help your consciousness to grow too.

Your soul: Your soul is an integral part of your consciousness, and your chakras serve as the main centers of the consciousness of your soul. There are seven main chakras in your body, and each chakra has a consciousness of its own. Reiki healing is concentrated on healing your chakras, as problems in your chakras will become evident much before the problems in your life are noticed. An understanding of the chakras can provide you an understanding of your life and hasten the healing process.

Your mind: You choose your thoughts, correct? Your mind is a part of your consciousness, and your thoughts reflect the feelings of love, wisdom, fear, and imbalance in your soul. You may choose to be guided by the divine guidance, and this puts you in tune with the universe. Practicing positive thoughts can not only help you speed up the healing process; it also enables you to attain enlightenment.

The Divine Guidance: Your divine guidance, the Absolute, or God—whatever you may wish to call it—is present with you at all times. It can anticipate each thought and each action that comes in your mind. Let your prayers and intent guide you toward the most wise and loving power.

Reincarnation: Your soul reincarnates as many times as it is guided by your actions and the divine guidance. It may have lived a hundred lives as a human, and there may be a period of review between various lifetimes in order to understand the learnings. It may also be guided to reincarnate immediately.

The Process of Healing

Reiki healing can never be misused or abused and is always used for the person's greatest benefit. Reiki power travels to the place where it is needed the most and does not need to be physically directed. It can work on every portion of the person—body, mind, soul, each and every chakra, every emotion, spirit, and karma. It can travel into the past, present, or the future. It can travel into each relationship, each incident, and each thought. All you need to do is trust this power. You should trust that this power is flowing to the place it is required the most. What happens in a scenario when you give Reiki healing to someone and that person does not need it? Since this power is never wasted, it is utilized at a later time.

Intent to Heal

Intent to heal is as simple as placing your hands on someone else or even yourself and letting the Reiki power flow through. A number of Reiki masters feel that it is imperative to request Reiki to flow as they begin a Reiki treatment. One of the most humble methods of requesting Reiki to flow is to develop a respect for yourself, Reiki, and the person receiving this Reiki healing energy.

Here are two ways to request the Reiki power to flow:

Method one: You may wish to bring your hands into the *Namaste* or folded-hands position (the position where your palms face toward each other and the five fingers on the left hand touch the five fingers on the right hand) and bow gently. You should then request the Reiki power to flow into and through you.

Method two: When you start the Reiki treatment, raise your hands above your head (position these in a manner that your palms face up) and then visualize the Reiki power flowing down from the heaven into your hands and then from your hands into and through your body.

An elaborate ceremony to facilitate the flow of Reiki is not required. Many times you may feel the need to help people with the flow of Reiki. In this scenario, all you need is their permission to place your hands on their body and channel the Reiki power to them. That is precisely the intent to heal that is required.

The first key of Reiki is surrender, which means you are just allowing Reiki to flow inside you and through you. It means that you are allowing Reiki to guide you and the receiver to receive the greatest possible healing benefits. You should remain aware and alert as you surrender yourself to the flow of the Reiki healing power. You surrender to the path of Reiki with willingness to let it flow in and through your body and a request to guide you.

Healing Your Own Self through Reiki or Unconditional Love

Your journey to self-healing begins with your **intent to heal**. You express an intention to find out more about yourself and experience healing and happiness through your commitment to change. You notice that big load being lifted from your shoulders through the trust that you placed in the divine guidance. This also gives you the confidence that you are moving in the right direction.

Through the healing process, you may experience feelings of sadness associated with deep pain or pure love and joy. Changes do happen in your life; you experience small and large changes, however, through self-healing. You also experience joy in each small change.

Here is a revelation: Prior to commencement of your Reiki self-healing journey, you were always engulfed by an armor that provided you an illusion of protection from your fears. The truth, however, is that this armor never protected you. In fact, it just served as a barrier that hampered your ability to experience life to the fullest because you were always engulfed with fear—fear that this armor was protecting you; this fear was always rooted deep inside you.

Taking off this armor enables you to breathe easily, to see clearly, and to experience the pleasures of the sunshine. And this sets you free from your self-imposed imprisonment. You let go of your fears and allow Reiki to heal you and to transform you.

Sometimes you suffer from some old wounds that are a result of the trauma that you experienced due to any past incident. Pain of separation from a loved one, failure in a specific life situation, and bereavement are some specific scenarios that impact individuals. As a result of a coping strategy that you may want to deploy, you sometimes close yourself from the world. This is nothing but a subconscious protective measure that you deploy. The pain from past experiences may stay buried deep inside you and sometimes exhibits itself as insecurity, unwillingness to give and receive love, and an inability to express certain kinds of emotions.

When you get attuned to Reiki, you discover the process of giving and receiving Reiki power to yourself and to others. You just need to use specific positions of your hands to heal you. This needs to be accompanied with your intent to heal, a commitment to change, and a willingness to progress.

Do make sure that you begin healing yourself through Reiki power with the same respect that you would demonstrate when you impart Reiki to another person. Place your hands into the folded-hands or *Namaste* position in front of your heart and bow gently. Then silently request the Reiki power to travel into and through you. You may request for your spiritual guides to be present in order to direct your treatment.

The basic hand positions are presented below for informational purposes only. Reiki should be practiced only after initiation by an authorized Reiki master.

- You should place one hand on your forehead and another on the back of your head (midway between the crown of the head and the base of the skull).
- You should then allow your hands to rest on your eyes.
- Next, you should leave your hands to rest on your ears.
- Then, you should place one of your hands on the upper chest area and the other hand below the solar plexus (below where your ribs come together).
- In the end, you should place your hands on your hip area.

You are advised to relax in each position for three to five minutes. Initially, you will have to practice these positions till you are familiar with each one of them. As stated earlier, you will need your guru to teach you and empower you with Reiki.

In the later stages, allow your intuition to guide you. A little patience and practice can lead you into a position where you just cannot commit any error. You should trust your intuition and the divine guidance. Your Reiki sessions can never be a waste as they are being observed by the divine force, which ensures that your efforts are always rewarded.

Healing Others through Selfless Love

It is not important to understand a person's values and beliefs in order to initiate the process of Reiki healing on him or her. However, knowing this does make a difference. Your feelings of compassion and love toward a particular person help in healing that person. At the same time, if somebody wishes to receive healing from you, your simple attitude of unconditional love helps the other person heal.

On receiving attunement to Reiki level one, you can help your friends and family by showering them with love, compassion, and attention. Before beginning the formal process of healing, it is important to create your sacred space. Always remember to wash your hands before and after the healing process.

You should explain to your recipient the complete process that you intend to follow. You should also let him or her know that Reiki power is an intelligent power and that he or she will receive the amount of power that he or she needs. Do not intrude into his or her space; seek permission to place your hands on his or her body. It is absolutely fine if your recipient sleeps during the process of receiving this Reiki power from you.

The following things are an important part of the healing process:

Developing a healthy attitude: Reiki believes in the power of positive affirmations. Before you start your journey, let yourself know that your recipient will be a healthier and a happier person. Counsel the recipient to let go of the past; he or she should let go of anything that has caused suffering and pain in the past and should be prepared to witness things in a whole new light.

Remember, **you only need love to heal**. You should be able to feel unconditional love for yourself and the person you are healing. You should also wish from your heart that the pain and suffering of your recipient should vanish. Tell yourself that the problems of your recipient are not your problems and you will not take them. Affirm that through the process of Reiki healing, the divine force will neutralize his or her pain and help him or her transform his or her life from darkness to light.

Tell yourself and the other person that the Reiki healing being provided to this person is for his or her greatest benefit, and always trust that the divine power is guiding you to facilitate the process of healing.

Creating a sacred space: During the process of healing, always try to create an environment that is free from any distraction or negative energy. Aim at creating a relaxing and comforting environment for your recipient. Always switch off your mobile phone, and place a "do not disturb" sign on the door of the room in which you plan to heal your patient. You can choose to play some gentle music that can calm your recipient during the healing process.

Once the process of healing is complete, it is a good idea to thank the sacred space.

Getting support: Before beginning any Reiki healing therapy, pray to the Absolute, the healers, the Reiki masters, and the Divine Spirit to support you and bless you with their divine guidance. Request their love, which can help you heal your recipient and guide him or her toward the path of eternal joy and happiness. Thank your God, your healer, your Reiki master, and the Divine Spirit for helping you with the healing process.

Enabling the Reiki power to flow: As you begin the process of Reiki healing, experience yourself as a divine being, as a part of God, and understand that by being a Reiki healer, you are being a channel for pure love because Reiki is nothing but love. Experience your heart chakra spinning around as you feel that unconditional love for everything. Visualize a magnificent ray of light entering into your head through your crown chakra and then moving down the other chakras into the heart chakra. Let this light now pass into your arms and then into each of the palms. Visualize that you are healing through your own love and the love of those who provide support to you. Understand that healing will happen, and also affirm that healing will be elevated by your intent to heal, your unconditional love, and your prayers for the healing process.

Placing your hands: During the healing process, you will need to place your hands on the other person's body. However, be very careful not to intrude into his or her personal space. Check with the recipient if he or she is comfortable with you placing your hands at certain positions on the body. Get your recipient's point of view on what is acceptable and what is not. Apply your discretion at certain places. An example could be that placement of your hand on the front chest may seem like a comfortable position for men. However, women may see this as an intrusion into their personal space.

The Reiki masters and advanced initiates of Reiki raja-yoga can transfer the Reiki power into your body from a distance as well without even physically touching you. Such is the versatility and power of this practice at higher levels.

Everything in this universe is connected: Everything in this universe originates from a single source and is therefore connected. This connection implies that you are permanently connected to everything, and it does not matter where it is. This connection empowers you to send Reiki power from one person to another, from one thing to the other, from something next door to something across the planet!

Healing from a distance: Reiki healing makes the process of healing from a distance possible. In order to provide Reiki healing to a person who is physically absent, you should just say a prayer to Reiki healers and request them to help to heal the other person. Do not imagine yourself to be present with the person; just feel the presence of your unconditional love for that person. Eliminate your emotions, boost your compassion and love for that person, and see yourself as a Reiki healer who can convey his or her love to the recipient. This will enable you and your recipient to experience that magic of Reiki healing.

Healing other things: When you decide to use Reiki, you also decide to bring that divine love on this planet. This love is used for the purpose of healing. You should aim at integrating Reiki with your daily life. You can Reiki your food, your medicines, your books, your machines—you can Reiki anything that is of prime importance to you. You just need to feel unconditional love toward everything.

Meditation: Meditation can be termed the process of channelizing your thoughts or turning your attention to a specific part of body, mind, or spirit inside or outside yourself. It plays an important role in self-healing and enables you to understand yourself and the divine guidance. It is a mechanism that allows you to build full concentration on a particular task and eliminate all distractions.

Try to make enough time for meditation. The recommended time is half an hour a day. Put out the dog, switch off your phone, and do everything else required to make sure that you do not get disturbed. Create your sacred space before you begin your meditation practice. Here is one of the simplest, yet most impactful, Reiki meditation techniques. This is called the Pink Lotus meditation:

STAGE 1

1. Be in the attitude of gratitude.
2. Take three (or seven) deep breaths.

3. Intend a pink lotus in your heart.
4. Intend that a joyous divine light of green color is entering your back heart chakra (from nature).
5. This energy provides nourishment to the lotus. The lotus expands and blooms.
6. *Be the lotus.* Feel how it is like being a lotus. This lotus is the symbol of divine love. Feel the peace, love, joy, and freedom.
7. Just be.

STAGE 2

1. Steps 1, 2, 3, and 4 are the same as above.
2. Intend a divine light of blue color is descending from the crown to the third eye-throat-heart into the lotus.
3. Steps 5, 6, and 7 are the same as above.

There is another meditation called *so-hum* breathing. This is a gentle shakti-based technique to reduce stress and take you deeper into the awareness of your self. It should be done on an empty stomach or at least one hour after a meal. You should sit on a firm floor or chair and keep your spine upright. This meditation can be done for fifteen to twenty minutes or for as long as you can comfortably do it.

1. When you breathe in, mentally or verbally chant, "Sooooooooooo."
2. When you breathe out, mentally or verbally chant, "Hummmmmmm."

This exercise will relax you and also take you into deeper levels of awareness. *So* means "like that," and *hum* means "I am." This exercise creates the awareness "I am that."

You Are the Transformation

By taking on the path toward self-healing via Reiki power, you are helping yourself and those around you. Your physical, emotional, mental, and spiritual growth ensure that you raise the level of consciousness in your own self and in other people. Here are some key things to be kept in mind as you give and receive Reiki and try to make this world a place full of love, compassion, and happiness:

- **Believe in yourself**: As a Reiki healer, you are a channel for heavenly love and healing. Spend time in healing yourself because this enables you to heal others.
- **Meditate**: Spend at least half an hour every day in meditation. This enhances your healing capabilities and helps you understand yourself.
- **Believe in the divine power**: Develop your faith; you are consciously being guided by a divine power that is wise, loving, intelligent, and conscious. This divine power is greater than anything else and guides and supports you; you may wish to call it God, Supreme, the Absolute, Divine Light, or anything that you choose!

Integrating Reiki into your daily life can enable you to reach your true potential and experience greater progress. Try to bring this goodness to the world by passing it to as many people as you can.

In today's world, lasting happiness is an achievement, and we all have the potential to achieve the same. In my realization, meditation (raja-yoga) combined with Reiki is the path and the vehicle to achieve eternal happiness. It also helps you become a happiness magnet or the change engine that transforms the world to greater happiness.

CHAPTER 9
Raja-Yoga

* * *

RAJA-YOGA IS OFTEN REFERRED TO as the royal path of meditation. Similar to a king who exercises control over his kingdom, you are expected to exercise control over the kingdom of your mind. The process of raja-yoga deploys your mental faculties to realize the *atman* or the self. This is accomplished through immense psychological control.

The foundation of raja-yoga rests on the fact that your awareness or perception of the divine self is masked as a result of the turbulences in your mind. The focus, therefore, has to be on the mind. If the mind can be controlled or made pure and still, the self shines.

> When, through the practice of yoga,
> the mind ceases its restless movements,
> and becomes still,
> the aspirant realizes the Atman. —*Bhagavad Gita*

Let me provide you a fair assessment of your present state of mind. Simply imagine a lake full of turbulence through speeding boats and waves. What would happen if this lake is also overloaded with pollution and gets a large number of visitors every single day? The lake would be full; it would appear chaotic and not so beautiful. That is the general state of your mind.

Let me now help you perform a simple activity.

I encourage you to leave everything aside at this very moment. This also means that you leave this book for five minutes (of course, after reading through the activity that you are to perform).

So, for five minutes sit quietly and meditate upon the *atman*. Take a stopwatch and time yourself.

I bet that during these five minutes, you were able to hear the sound of that buzzing fly more clearly. You also began to wonder about breakfast or dinner. Some of you may have also made grocery lists in your mind. You could have even figured out where you left your car keys. In fact, some of you may have reflected upon how your yesterday went and drawn certain definite conclusions from the happenings.

Therefore, the very attempt to *meditate* ensured that there were many thoughts entering and exiting your mind at the same time—the thought of lost keys, the thought of yesterday's heated argument, the thought of dinner, the thought of grocery shopping, the thought of too many flies buzzing around…As one thought stopped, another one jumped in with a lot more force.

In the hustle and bustle of your everyday life, you are not even aware of these erratic movements in your mind. You have become habituated to this mental churning. The constant wandering of your mind is not an area of concern for you.

This is similar to parents who have not been able to discipline their children. These children begin to trouble people around them.

Similarly, failure to discipline the mind can lead to an ill-mannered mind, which only creates difficulties for you and the people around you. Lack of psychological discipline ensures that you suffer loads of mental agony and remain unhappy.

Now, for a moment, forget about that turbulent lake and visualize a beautiful, clear lake. There is absolutely no pollution, and the lake is not overloaded with visitors. There are no speeding boats and rafts. In fact, the waves have also settled down.

How do you feel about it?

Try looking down. You can even see the bottom of the lake.

This bottom of the lake can be compared to the *atman* that resides deep within your personality. A pure mind empowers you to look at your true self. It cannot remain hidden from you. And raja-yoga believes that this mind can be yours. **You can be the master of this mind.**

The science of raja-yoga empowers you with the knowledge that enables you to observe your internal state. If you are able to guide your power of attention and direct it toward the internal world, you will be able to analyze your mind and get enlightened with some facts.

You could compare the immense power of mind to rays of bright light. These rays are of absolutely no good if they are dissipated.

However, if all these rays combine together to become concentrated on one single place or object, they illuminate that place or object.

Ever since you were born, society taught you to concentrate your attention on external things. This is natural; it happens to every child who is born. Talking about the impact this has on the child, this child grows up to be an individual who loses the basic ability of observing his or her internal mechanism. He or she is not able to concentrate and therefore does not understand his or her true nature. Meditation and analysis of the mind seem to be a really tedious job. However, that is the only scientific approach to understanding the self and, in the journey, attaining true unconditional happiness.

The analysis of mind imparts to a human the knowledge that the self cannot be destroyed and that it is perfect and pure. This brings in lasting happiness and comfort.

Most of the time, misery is a result of fear of the unknown. When, through the path of raja-yoga, a human discovers that he or she cannot be destroyed, that he or she will never die, the fear of death vanishes. The knowledge that you are perfect is realized through the path of raja-yoga, and this knowledge leads to demolition of all vain desires. This ensures that there is no misery, only perfect bliss!

The single most effective method to attain this profound knowledge is called concentration.

The chef in the kitchen concentrates his or her knowledge on the recipe being prepared and throws in all the required ingredients. The chemist in a laboratory concentrates his or her knowledge on the experiment, throws in the required chemicals, and draws certain conclusions. The chef is successful in creating a mouthwatering dish, and the chemist is successful in discovering certain secrets. The ingredients in the recipe and the chemicals in the laboratory ensure that they give out their secrets to the chef and the chemist respectively.

I urge you to draw upon the faculty of concentration because the more you concentrate on what I have to say, the better your grasp of the subject. In fact, the more I concentrate my powers on the things that I have to teach you, the better I will be able to teach you.

The most powerful secret of the human mind is concentration. The science of concentration ensures that the mind achieves maximum power.

Quite often you work and think at the same time. This is because you are not able to concentrate your efforts on one thing at a time. The art of concentration can ensure that your mind is able to penetrate its own deep-rooted secrets.

The science of raja-yoga teaches you to concentrate your mind, discover your innermost secrets, and draw your own conclusions. It is a long and difficult path that takes years of dedicated effort and patience to master—but when you master this science, you develop an understanding of yourself. You develop an understanding between your mind and body, and you learn to exercise control over your mind.

A part of this science is physical, but the greater and more important part is the mental part, the art of concentration.

Raja-yoga helps you attain control over your body and mind so that you are able to train your mind as and when required, bring it under your control, ensure that it works in the manner you want it to work, and force it to concentrate its powers where they are needed the most.

According to raja-yoga, the external world is simply the consequence of your internal world. Whatever goes inside your mind impacts your outside world. This also means that if you learn to control your mind or your internal world, you will get the entire world of nature under your control. The laws of nature will have no influence on you, and you will be able to go beyond them.

The ultimate aim of Yoga is unity. Raja-yoga begins from the internal world, studies the laws related to the external world, and through this knowledge, is able to control the external and the internal world.

There is no mystery in what I teach through this book or through the various courses at the Divine Heart Center. I want to give to you all that I have received through my self-realization. However, I urge you to make your own discoveries as well through regular and disciplined practice. Raja-yoga is a science that should be studied like any other science. Nothing is hidden or mysterious in this science, but you have to experience it yourself.

Let me now talk about the *Samkhya* philosophy. It is important to understand the Samkhya philosophy before getting into the details of raja-yoga.

THE SAMKHYA PHILOSOPHY

The Samkhya philosophy was founded by a great Indian sage, Kapila. The word *Samkhya* is derived from a Sanskrit word, *Samkhya*, which means number. If we break up the word *Samkhya*, *Sam* implies harmony, balance, and equality, and *khya* means wisdom, knowledge, and understanding.

Samkhya is dualistic in nature and advocates two realities: the *purusha* (self or spirit) and the *prakriti* (matter).

Prakriti is considered as the primal cause of the natural world. It is also the cause of experiences related to matter and energy. It is different from consciousness. Everything that we perceive evolves from *prakriti*. This also implies that anything that is the source of our anger, pain, pleasure, hatred, or love evolves from *prakriti*. It is something that cannot be altered and remains unchanged.

Purusha is regarded as the observer. He is pure consciousness or pure witness. *Purusha* is the unchanging witness of *prakriti*.

The single goal of the Samkhya philosophy is freedom from all suffering. An individual desires to get rid of his or her mind or body if the pain within is immense and deep. Since he or she is unaware of the process of separating his or her body and mind from his or her self and becoming a pure consciousness, he or she gets disturbed and experiences more pain.

The Samkhya philosophy acknowledges the actual experience of pain, pleasure, anger, and hatred and lays down a framework for removing this. Samkhya's belief in the principle of cause and effect tells us that we can go backward, remove the cause, and in the process eliminate the effect. It is simple: remove the cause of sorrow, and the effect is eliminated.

Freedom from pain leads a person to experience a sense of pure being or *kaivalya*.

Let us look at the three kinds of pain and suffering and the methodology to attain freedom from these according to the Samkhya philosophy:

PHYSICAL PAIN:
Physical suffering can be prevented by a balanced behavior, proper exercise, proper diet, sleeping on time, and waking up on time. In order to relieve oneself from physical pain, Samkhya views Ayurveda as an important tool.

EMOTIONAL OR PSYCHOLOGICAL PAIN:
A person who is experiencing emotional or psychological pain needs help from outside (body) and inside (mind). Psychological support can

be created through self-belief and trust. The first four steps of raja-yoga are an important tool here. I will discuss these steps later in this chapter. These can be used in conjunction with certain external measures (Ayurveda) to improve the physical symptoms and relieve overall sorrow and grief.

SPIRITUAL PAIN:
According to the Samkhya philosophy, spiritual pain can be overcome by deep diving into one's own self and understanding his or her pure being. The last four limbs of raja-yoga help in achieving this state by eliminating all that is nonessential or not a part of pure self.

You are a blend of the material world and pure consciousness. Although pure consciousness is something to aspire for, you should not condemn the part of the body that is not pure consciousness.

Everything that has been created around you has a purpose; the purpose is to provide you the tools to overcome all types of pain and suffering, achieve holistic happiness, and experience your pure being. Your creation is not an accident, and therefore life should not be viewed as a punishment. Life in itself is an opportunity for you to understand pain, suffering, joy, and sorrow again and again. Your ultimate goal in life is to free yourself from this cycle of pain, suffering, and sorrow.

The Samkhya philosophy believes in a world where you live in an integrated manner—where *prakriti* (shakti) and *purusha* (*shiva*) walk hand in hand and help each other achieve a common goal. *Prakriti* is unable to see, but has the power to move. *Purusha* is unable to move, but has the power to see.

You need to work through integration of your consciousness, body, breath, and mind in order to achieve one common goal—holistic happiness. The integration of Reiki with raja-yoga is instrumental in helping you achieve this goal.

THE EIGHT STEPS OF RAJA-YOGA
Raja-yoga is divided into eight steps.

STEP ONE: YAMA OR SELF-CONTROL
This comprises five basic principles:

1. **Ahimsa or nonviolence**: *Ahimsa* or nonviolence means "not to kill" and "not to cause pain to anyone by word, thought, or deed." Most Raja yogis are vegetarians, and *ahimsa* is the prime reason behind that. Consumption of nonvegetarian food means killing of an animal. The animal senses when it is going to be slaughtered (due to the instincts it possesses). As a consequence, stress hormones are released in the animal's body. These stress hormones remain in the flesh of the dead animal and are consumed by humans. This is the origin of anxiety, depression, psychosis, neurosis, and so on in some human beings.
2. **Satya or truthfulness**: It is important to speak the truth. However, it is more important to speak the truth with love. Speaking the truth all the time also means that you do not hide your feelings. Always remember that no matter how much you try to hide your feelings, there is one observer you cannot hide these from—your own inner self! Your consciousness is always a witness to how you feel.
3. **Asteya or nonstealing**: This means that you should refrain from taking or using anything that does not belong to you. This principle not only applies to physical objects, but also applies

to mental images or feelings. This is the reason why we say that you must not steal hope, joy, or opportunity from a person.
4. **Brahmacharya or the practice of a pure way of life**: A number of people view *brahmacharya* as sexual abstinence. In reality, *brahmacharya* is much more than that. It is the awareness about the Divine. It does not mean that you must neglect your worldly duties. It only means that you perform all your duties with the feeling that the Divine is the doer and you are merely acting as per the will of the Divine.
5. **Aparigraha or nonaccumulation of worldly possessions**: A person who owns a lot of worldly things also owns a lot of worry. Therefore, you must only possess what you need and require. All excess must be let go of. This is true as a part of your general nature as well. You must not hold on to a particular person. Letting go ensures that you are free as well.

Step two: Niyama or discipline

This comprises five basic principles:

1. **Shauca or purity**: This principle emphasizes external and internal purity. Everything that you associate with should be pure. This implies your clothes, body, feelings, thoughts, and the people you associate yourself with. In order to attain maximum spiritual benefits, it is advisable to be in company of people who can influence you in a positive manner.
2. **Santosh or contentment**: The realization that all worldly goods are a cause of disappointment and inner wealth is the only wealth that can make you experience true, holistic happiness brings in the feeling of contentment or *santosh*.
3. **Tapa or self-discipline**: The only key to success is self-control, determination, perseverance, and patience. Exhibiting full

control over yourself, you must continue on your chosen path even when life throws challenges in the form of obstacles.
4. **Svadhyaya or study of scriptures**: The ancient yoga scriptures, such as the *Yoga Sutra* by Patanjali, the *Upanishads*, *Bhagavad Gita*, and so on, impart a wealth of knowledge related to yoga and must be studied consistently.
5. **Ishvara pranidhana or devotion toward God**: Surrender yourself to the Divine. The Divine will protect you from all evil.

STEP THREE: ASANA OR PHYSICAL EXERCISES

You must perform a series of mental and physical exercises every day until you reach that higher state. The easiest posture should be chosen first, and you must be able to retain it for a long time. Whatever posture you choose, you must ensure that your spinal cord is held free—your neck, chest, and head must be in a straight line. Your ribs must be able to hold the entire weight of your body. The aim of this step is to enable you to establish control over your physical and mental self. You must acquire control over all the muscles in your body. With practice, you will be able to even control your heart.

Practice is absolutely important. Merely reading this book or listening to me will not make things happen. You will have to practice every day. You will have to see, feel, and experience things. You may sometimes feel doubtful of the whole process. However, with experience, you will be able to notice positive changes, and this will give you faith and encouragement.

Imagine yourself practicing to concentrate your thoughts on the tip of your nostrils. With practice, you will be able to smell the finest of fragrances. However, that should not be your ultimate aim. Your main goal or ultimate aim is to achieve holistic happiness through liberation of your soul. For this purpose, you must strive to achieve absolute control over nature.

Step four: Pranayama

Pranayama, in the deepest sense of the word, is extraction of prana from this universe. It implies that you understand the *ayam* (or the dimension) of prana. For example, the sun is the largest source of new prana on this planet. But when you look at the sun, you see a celestial body burning heat and light.

However, a yogi does not look at the sun that way. A yogi looks at the sun as a *devta* or a conscious being, and the yogi looks at the light of the sunrays as a conscious energy or conscious prana. And this is the difference between science and spirituality. This is also the difference between some folks that practice yoga in the West versus the Eastern yogi; the Eastern yogi sees the nature or sun as life and worships the sun as a source of this living or as the intelligent life force. Through the practice of *pranayama*, the yogi is able to extract prana from the universe and circulate it inside his or body—balance it and purify it to his or her maximum benefit. That is the true purpose of *pranayama*.

In simple terms, *pranayama* means gaining control over your breathing. *Pranayama* must be practiced twice daily—early morning and toward early evening. Try to create a room for this practice. Do not sleep in this room, and enter it only when you have bathed and are ready to practice. Let no unholy or angry thoughts gain entry into that room.

Sit in a straight posture and begin the process by sending some holy thoughts to all creation. Tell yourself that you wish all beings to be happy, peaceful, and healthy. The easiest way to achieve happiness is by seeing others happy. Next, view your own body as strong and healthy, believe in the power of your mind, and notice how it works miracles for you.

A number of people view *pranayama* as control of breath. That is only a part of the picture. The main focus of *pranayama* is control over your prana. Breath is simply a vehicle that helps in transport of prana in and out of your body. Balancing this prana can lead to an overall harmonious body and mind that has the capability to heal itself—physically, mentally, emotionally, and spiritually.

Knowledge and control of prana can bring unlimited power.

The *Vedas* have generalized the entire universe into one Absolute. Any person who has understood this Absolute has also understood the universe. Similarly, all the forces of nature are generalized into prana. If you are able to understand prana, you are also able to understand the physical and the mental forces of the universe. You are then able to control your body and the mind.

The initiation of *pranayama* begins with trying to gain control over things that are near you. In the human body, the most important display of prana can be through the control of the motion of the lungs.

If lungs stop functioning, the body will stop functioning. However, certain people are able to train themselves in a manner that their body continues to live even when the motion in lungs has stopped. Some Raja yogis have been known to bury themselves for days and continue to live without breathing.

Pranayama means controlling this motion of lungs, and this motion is associated with breath. Breath is not producing this motion. In fact, it is this motion that produces breath. The pumping action of the lungs draws in the air. The prana moves the lungs, and this movement of lungs pulls in the air. Therefore, we can safely say that *pranayama* is not breathing. It is controlling the muscular power that moves the lungs. The muscular power is the prana, and this is what needs to be controlled through the practice of *pranayama*.

The power of the human mind is such that it can control each and every muscle in the body. You cannot move your ears. However, animals can. The reason you cannot do this is not because you do not have the power to do so, but because you have never exercised that power.

Practice and hard work can ensure that you are able to control those motions of the body that are most dormant. Have you heard that during the practice of *pranayama*, you must fill your whole body with prana? A number of people think about this as breath. However, this is the life-force energy. When you fill your whole body with prana or life-force energy, you develop the potential to control the entire body. You can then control the misery and the tension that engulf you and ensure that you achieve only what you deserve—holistic happiness!

Many times within your own body, the supply of prana gravitates toward one particular part. You notice that a part of your body seems healthier than another. This is because of the inconsistent supply of prana. The part of the body where the supply is diminished seems to be unhealthy or diseased.

Raja-yoga can provide you the power to control your prana. With practice, you will be able to control your prana and understand where you need to concentrate it. So, you may be able to figure out that your toe has less prana than the hand, and raja-yoga combined with Reiki can ensure that you send the requisite amount of prana to your toe. By concentrating your energies, you can master your prana. Engaging in the act of meditation also implies that you are concentrating on the prana.

Let me take the example of a vast ocean here. The ocean has little bubbles, which merge into giant waves that once again merge into the vast ocean. The wave connects the bubble to the ocean. Similarly, humans could be like a gigantic wave or a small bubble; all humans are connected by the infinite ocean of energy. The storehouse of this infinite energy lies behind every living being.

Living beings evolve—from a little fungus to forms such as plants, animals, humans, and ultimately the Divine. This is attained through millions and trillions of years.

A Raja yogi has the power to shorten this time span. He or she can in fact lessen this time span to six years or maybe six months…the possibilities are endless! It depends on you; you decide the time that you want to take in order to gain infinite knowledge, wisdom, and power.

The complete science of raja-yoga is directed at teaching people how through the power of assimilation you can reach a point of perfection (and that too in a short period of time). This is what all sages, prophets, and great men do. *They concentrate—strengthen the power of assimilation—and in the process shorten the time required to achieve perfection, holistic happiness, and ultimately self-realization.*

The part of *pranayama* that attempts to control the physical aspect of prana is often referred to as physical science. The part that attempts to control the demonstration of prana as a mental force through mental means is termed raja-yoga.

Step five: Pratyahara or withdrawal of senses
A Raja yogi possesses the power to withdraw his or her senses and direct his or her mind at will. This is similar to a tortoise, who has the

power to withdraw its limbs under its shell and extend them out when needed again.

You can obtain complete independence from external conditions when you are able to practice controlled *pratyahara*. The first stage involves meditation by keeping your eyes closed, your body motionless, and thoughts directed inward.

As a child is born, he or she is taught to be good and kind, abstain from stealing, and so on. However, he or she is not taught **how** to abstain from stealing or be good to others. He or she is simply told about it. This will not help, unless he or she understands how to control the mind.

Actions are a result of your mind connecting itself to certain centers termed the organs. This becomes the reason why people commit acts of foolishness at times. Bringing the mind under control can prevent this. Misery and pain can be denied if your mind becomes strong enough to ignore these senses.

When you are successful in detaching your mind from the centers, and that too at your own will, you are successful in achieving *pratyahara*.

Your mind is like an untamed monkey. The first step to control it depends on your knowledge and understanding of the things it is capable of doing when not in control. Sit for some time and allow your mind to run. You will be astonished at the number of thoughts that you think during this time. When you consciously perform this exercise every day, you notice that your days become calmer, and the mind stops wandering.

So, for the first few months, you will notice loads of thoughts in the mind, and then slowly, these thoughts will become fewer. Over a period of time, you will be able to control your mind at your will.

The only key to achieving this state is consistent practice every day. You must practice this every day in order to achieve a state where the mind is in your control and you do not allow it to join any other center. This is the state of *pratyahara*.

You must move to the next step (*dharana* or concentration) only after you have practiced *pratyahara* for a few months and mastered it.

STEP SIX: DHARANA OR CONCENTRATION

Dharana or concentration is the art of holding your mind to certain points. So, you force your mind to feel certain parts of the body as opposed to others. An example could be you feeling only your left foot as opposed to other parts of your body.

You are trying to confine your chitta or the mind to a limited place. This *dharana* or the practice of concentration is of various kinds. For example, you can feel just your heart. If this seems difficult, you can feel a lotus in place of your heart. Gradually, you will be able to feel rays of effulgent light in the lotus.

As a Raja yogi, you must continue to practice. During your practice, you must refrain from speaking with others and try to be alone. This is only to ensure that you are not distracted during your practice session.

With practice, even the sound of a pin dropping appears like a thunderbolt. As practice gets deeper, perceptions become finer.

Begin with listening to someone who has achieved realization (your guru); understand what he or she says, and then begin your practice.

Leave all distractions and focus on concentrating your mind. You must concentrate to develop the truth inside you. Pick up one thing and finish till the end. Do not get distracted and give up in between—not until you have seen the end.

As a Raja yogi, pick up an idea and make it your life. Live that idea, breathe that idea, talk that idea—let every part of your body experience that idea. This is the only methodology to success, and this is the methodology that produces great spiritual leaders. This is the only way to achieve holistic happiness and progress toward self-realization.

Do not let your mind get disturbed, try to be in the company of some really good people, choose your guru carefully, and practice hard. If you are determined, you will experience your transition into a Raja yogi in around six months. However, if spiritualism and philosophy are only viewed as objects of entertainment, then you will not make any progress. A great amount of perseverance and willpower is needed to succeed.

You cannot master *dharana* until you become capable of concentrating your thoughts on a particular object.

Step seven: Dhyana or meditation

The meditative state can be called the highest state of existence. All meditative techniques only serve as preliminary exercise to reach this state.

Reaching this state requires an immense amount of practice and perseverance. When you are there through perseverance and practice, you are able to experience your true self. This is the time when you notice that your individual ego ceases to exist and you become one with the Absolute.

The practice of meditation begins with gross objects and eventually rises to finer objects, until it becomes objectless at a point. You must first deploy your mind in perception of external causes of sensation, then the internal motion, and eventually, your own reaction.

When you succeed in perceiving the external causes of sensation, your mind also acquires the power to perceive all internal motion, and then you develop control over the mental waves. You decide if you will allow any thoughts to enter your mind or not and, in case you allow thoughts, what they would be. This is the state where a yogi acquires knowledge of everything. Every thought that enters a yogi's mind is a result of the power that the mind acquires. A yogi develops control over this mind and experiences his or her pure being. This is when he or she experiences the divine light shining within his or her heart.

STEP EIGHT: THE STATE OF SAMADHI OR COMPLETE REALIZATION
This is the state where the knowledge, object of knowledge, and the knower unite.

When you eat food, you do it consciously. When you assimilate food, you do it unconsciously. The process where this food provides strength to the body is also accomplished unconsciously.

The assimilation of food, as well as the process where food provides strength to your body, is also performed by you. There cannot be a separate person inside you to perform this task. So, how are you performing these tasks then?

You are performing these tasks unconsciously.

Through *dhyana* and *samadhi*, it is possible to bring every unconscious action to a conscious plane.

Today, if I ask you to control your heart, you would probably not be able to do so. However, with practice, you can bring every part of your body under your control.

Your mind works in two planes. The plane of consciousness has ego attached to it. The unconscious plane is devoid of feelings of egoism.

There is another higher plane that can go beyond consciousness; it is called the superconscious plane. The unconscious plane is below the conscious plane, and the superconscious plane is above the conscious plane. The feelings of "I," "me," and "mine" are almost abolished in the planes above and below the conscious plane but in a very different way.

Samadhi helps a person achieve the state of superconsciousness (reaching the higher plane).

A person can enter deep sleep and reach the plane of unconsciousness. Here, he or she will not know that his or her heart is beating and he or she is breathing and performing all other functions that are so vital for survival. He or she will get up and become the same conscious human. There will not be any enhancement in knowledge, and hence, he or she will not achieve enlightenment. This is not *samadhi*.

Going into the plane of superconsciousness is *samadhi*. A person who enters *samadhi* as a fool is bound to come out as a sage.

Let us now look at the practical application of *samadhi*. The conscious workings of the human mind are limited. The mind tries to reason everything. There are certain questions such as "Is God there?" "Am I a soul?" or "Is there some supreme intelligence that guides this universe?"

Such questions are beyond the field of reason. But you still need an answer.

There is only one answer to this—*that this world is only a tiny drop in the mighty ocean; it is just a small link in the infinite chain.*

If you ask a sage or a prophet where he or she got all those answers from, the most probable reply would be that he or she met an angel in the form of a human being, or that he or she dreamed of an ancestor telling him or her the answers, or that his or her guru came in his or her dreams and ensured that he or she had all the answers.

The only common thing here is that all these prophets and sages gathered knowledge and that this knowledge came from beyond reasoning. This was the knowledge that was present within them; hence, it appeared from inside them!

That is the state of *samadhi*. It teaches that your mind has a higher state of existence, a state beyond reason. It is a superconscious state, and when your mind reaches this higher state, you are empowered with knowledge.

The various steps in yoga are designed to scientifically bring you into this superconscious state or *samadhi*. Everybody must strive to reach this state.

Samadhi is achieved when the mind does not need any basis to concentrate; it just becomes one wave.

If you can fix your mind on a center for twelve seconds, you reach the state of *dharana*. Twelve such *dharanas* become *dhyana*, and twelve *dhyanas* combine to become a *samadhi*.

Samadhi is further divided into two kinds: *samprajnata* (where you develop the power to control nature) and *asamprajnata* (where through the constant cessation of mental activity, the chitta retains the unexhibited impressions).

Achieving the state of *samadhi* is pure bliss. In this state, all previous tendencies of dullness and restlessness are destroyed. All tendencies of goodness are also destroyed. The omnipresent soul is left alone, and people understand that they are neither born nor do they die. They understand that it was not they who came and went; it was nature that was moving, and this movement was reflected upon the soul.

The state of *samadhi* ensures that one unites with the Divine. You become a river that unites with the ocean after a long and tiresome journey. You become one with your consciousness.

Your free soul is in a position to command, it does not beg or pray, and all its desires are immediately fulfilled.

The Samkhya philosophy is theist in that it accepts the authority of the *Vedas*. However, the Samkhya philosophy believes that there is no one God. When everybody is a soul, God should also be a soul. And if God were a soul, how would he have the power to create?

Kapila, the founder of the Samkhya philosophy, mentions that there are many souls, and the minds of a number of perfect souls merge together, only to reemerge as masters. These are the gods. In time, we shall all become such gods.

While Samkhya philosophy is important to understand for you to be able to understand the framework on which the system of yoga is based, it is not my intention in this book to debate the existence or nonexistence of one God. I have a very unique viewpoint based on my direct realization in meditation that the seekers' perception of God changes as they progress in their own meditation. Initially they may see themselves as different from God because there is a difference between their realization and the realization that exists outside of this creation.

I believe in the philosophy of *Advait Vedant,* which is a nondualistic philosophy or the culmination of the *Vedas,* which talks about the Absolute as *Brahm,* the being as the *Jeeva,* and the cosmic illusion that separates the two as maya. This cosmic illusion creates the sense of separateness between us and the Absolute. Through the process of yoga, this sense of separateness can be removed, and the Absolute starts manifesting in your own self. That is where in my mind the Samkhya philosophy starts uniting with the *Advait Vedant* philosophy.

However, I am not really a theoretical scholar. I am a Yogi, and I primarily talk in depth about things that I experience and believe in. I have used the texts for encouragement and direction, but ultimately, I put the practices of Reiki Raja Yoga to test by practicing them regularly, and through those practices my realization and experience of the Absolute and different stages of *samadhi* continue to expand. This is what I expect of you as well.

Whether you believe in God or do not believe in God, the practice of Reiki raja-yoga will support you and take you off from wherever you are. It will empower you to experience a deeper understanding of your own self and of the Absolute. The self-effort part of what I teach during the daily practice, the *pranyamas,* the meditations, the Reiki healings—all are in line with the Samkhya philosophy of self-effort.

The surrender portions of Reiki and yoga are in line with that higher power whose grace we all need and without which nothing is possible.

And you want the grace from the highest source—the Absolute.

So, the practice of Reiki and raja-yoga supports any or all true philosophies about God and places emphasis on your own direct realization. Find out for yourself; develop clarity through your own practice under the guidance of a guru.

ENDING EACH STEP THINKING ABOUT THE ONE ABSOLUTE

In India, it is common for every family to have an *Ishta Devata*. This *Ishta Devata* becomes your favorite form of visualizing the Divine. This form could be anything or anyone; it is dependent on the religious traditions and values that you are raised with.

In raja-yoga, it is very important to conclude each step with visualization of this *Ishta Devata*. You could decide who your *Ishta Devata* would be; it could simply be a beautiful landscape or a lotus emanating light. It could also be a simple source of light that signifies unison with the Divine.

CHAPTER 10

The Crème de la Crème of Raja-Yoga: Kriya Yoga

✳ ✳ ✳

THE TERM *KRIYA* MEANS "ACTION" (to do, act, or react), and the term *yoga* implies integration (union). Therefore, *kriya yoga* would mean unification of consciousness (which is a result of the unending movement of your thoughts) with spiritual awakening (which sets you free from all mental distractions). You may even call it the union of self with the Absolute through a particular action.

Kriya deconditions the mind and, in the process, sets you free from your past karma. It possesses the power to provide a subtle universal uniqueness to your ego center, which then transforms it to bring immense harmony in your life.

Kriya yoga can be termed a unique combination of *hatha yoga, raja-yoga, and Laya yoga*. With practice, you tend to settle in your natural state, and your body then acts on signals received only from its own chakras. In this state, no thoughts interfere, and hence there is no scope for any psychosomatic pursuits and problems.

It is a simple method that decarbonizes the human brain and recharges it with oxygen. This ensures that the yogi converts his or her cells into pure energy.

This is referenced in the *Bhagavad Gita* by Sri Krishna as:

> Offering inhaling breath into the outgoing breath, and offering the outgoing breath into the inhaling breath, the yogi neutralizes both these breaths; he thus releases the life force from the heart and brings it under his control.

Swami Paramhansa Yogananda interprets it as:

> The yogi arrests decay in the body by an addition of life force, and arrests the mutations of growth in the body by apan (eliminating current). Thus neutralizing decay and growth, by quieting the heart, the yogi learns life control.

The great yoga guru Patanjali mentions *kriya yoga* as a combination of mental control, body discipline, and meditation on aum.

Swami Paramhansa Yogananada also mentions that

> The Kriya Yogi mentally directs his life energy to revolve, upward and downward, around the six spinal centers (medullary, cervical, dorsal, lumbar, sacral, and coccygeal plexuses) which correspond to the twelve astral signs of the zodiac, the symbolic Cosmic Man. A half minute of revolution of energy around the sensitive spinal cord of man effects subtle progress in his evolution; that half minute of Kriya equals one year of natural spiritual unfoldment.

> The astral system of a human being, with six (twelve by polarity) inner constellations revolving around the sun of the omniscient spiritual eye, is interrelated with the physical sun and the twelve zodiacal signs. All men are thus affected by an inner and an outer universe. The ancient rishis discovered that man's earthly

and heavenly environment, in twelve-year cycles, push him forward on his natural path. The scriptures aver that man requires a million years of normal, diseaseless evolution to perfect his human brain sufficiently to express cosmic consciousness.

One thousand Kriya practiced in eight hours gives the yogi, in one day, the equivalent of one thousand years of natural evolution: 365,000 years of evolution in one year. In three years, a Kriya Yogi can thus accomplish by intelligent self-effort the same result which nature brings to pass in a million years. The Kriya short cut, of course, can be taken only by deeply developed yogis.

These yogis are guided by their gurus, and they are able to prepare their minds and bodies to receive the power that is created through intensive practice.

Today, a number of self-proclaimed Godmen and yogis try to teach forceful holding of breath in the lungs. This is considered to be a part of breathing exercises.

However, *kriya yoga* is a science and does not propagate this. From beginning to end, *kriya* is about peace and believes in converting breath into mind.

It believes that breath control is mind control, and the state of breathlessness is considered as deathlessness. This is the ultimate state of *samadhi*, where you become one with the Absolute.

Through the process of *kriya*, the outgoing life force is never wasted. It is rather controlled so that it can be combined with subtler spinal energies. The process of *kriya yoga* ensures that the life-force energy feeds all the cells of the body and mind, and therefore they remain in a magnetized state.

This ancient science is based on almost all forms of mental and physical exercises. It enables you to attain freedom from death. As a *kriya yogi*, your life is never influenced by past actions, but always through the guidance that you receive through your soul. The pure fire of *yoga* leads to eternal radiance, and through devoted practice, you become one with the Absolute.

Traditionally, *kriya yoga* is divided into six stages as first kriya, second kriya, and so on. As a beginner, you begin with first kriya and gradually move to the higher levels.

The Divine Heart Center conducts guided meditations and initiation seminars on *kriya yoga* regularly. I invite you to one of our retreats to witness the magic yourself. Elevated energy levels, physical healing, emotional balancing, inner stability, strength, and peace are only some of the benefits that you would experience.

The techniques taught include *kriya yoga pranayama breathing, kriya yoga asanas, kriya meditation,* and *kriya mantras (sacred sound syllables)*. These will gradually elevate your consciousness and awareness level to a point where you become one with the Absolute. The powerful integration of *kriya yoga* with Reiki will awaken your kundalini and help in self-realization.

CHAPTER 11
Integrating Reiki and Raja-Yoga

*   *   *

INTEGRATING REIKI AND RAJA-YOGA IS extremely important as it is through this integration that prana and prema, kundalini and kripa, and the path of shakti and bhakti combine. The divine grace descends through the *antahkarana* into the being through Reiki, which cleans up the chakras and nadis, including sushumna. This is when the kundalini fire automatically ascends the spine. Through the use of kriya techniques, another boost is given to kundalini *Devi*, and she rises and evolves faster, burning karma and samskaras at a much faster rate.

Reiki dissolves karma like water, and kundalini burns karma like fire. The combination of the two is the most potent in this universe for spiritual and material progress. Materially, it can be understood that you become unconditional in your love and unlimited in your willpower.

The table below provides a comparison between integrated Reiki raja-yoga practice and the traditional Reiki and kriya yoga practices. This is by no means to say that traditional Reiki and kriya practices are not powerful practices. The practice of Reiki raja-yoga has a wider applicability and can fit a wider variety of lifestyles and spiritual pursuits. Kriya yoga is the most powerful practice available to humankind to realize the Absolute.

Category	Traditional Reiki	Traditional Kriya Yoga	Reiki Raja-Yoga
Ultimate goal	• Happiness and abundance in life	• Self-realization by the vision of the Kuthastha Chaitanya • Achieve no mind and, ultimately, "no breath" state of *samadhi*	• Self-realize while achieving happiness and abundance in life (raja yogi) • For most: create happiness within one's world and worldwide • For some: achieve no mind and, ultimately, "no breath" state of *samadhi* • For a few: merge into the Absolute.

Primary power	*Kripa* or divine grace	Kundalini or divine willpower	Divine grace as well as divine willpower
Nature	• Para-shakti; beyond power or the personal power of the Absolute • Para-shakti is the controller of param shakti.	• Param-shakti; supreme power of the Absolute as Ishwar or the Lord	• Both para-shakti and param shakti
Base mantras	• "Nam Myoho Renge Kyo." I fully accept the karmic law of the Divine.	• Aum or divine word	• "Aum. Prem. Brahm" or "Divine Word. Divine Love. Divine, the Absolute."

Initiation	• Connects the seeker to divine grace; initiation happens from the crown chakra down through the *antahkarana* or the pillar of light (top-down empowerment).	Awakens the kundalini by infusion of higher prana by the will of the guru; initiation lifts the kundalini from the root chakra upward through the Sushumna nadi (bottom-up empowerment)	• A dual initiation happens, whereby (1) divine grace is requested to enter from the crown chakra downward through the *antahkaran*, and (2) the path of kundalini is cleared from the root chakra upward through sushumna. • Both top-down and bottom-up initiation is achieved. • The initiate experiences faster spiritual and material balance based on his or her starting point and the quality of his or her surrender.

| Asanas and overall practice | • Doesn't require specific *asanas*—most poses can be adjusted to fit one's physical ability. Most techniques can be done while lying down; many can be done while traveling in a vehicle. Most techniques don't require an empty stomach.
• Touch healing is the hallmark practice, but healing remotely using distant healing is also practiced. | • All techniques require the seeker to sit with spine straight and avoid back support for energy to flow freely in the spine. Most techniques require an empty stomach (before meals or three hours after meals). Kriya is advised not to be done during a thunderstorm. Facing east during meditation is recommended.
• Kriya yogis can spiritually heal with mantras and willpower | • A combination of techniques from Reiki and raja-yoga provide a flexible yet intense practice. which can be done twenty-four hours a day even by a busy professional and even while traveling. Two to three hours of practice can be accommodated without making drastic changes to one's schedule. Techniques can be selected based on one's own capacity and desire to progress. |

			without physical touch (distant healing).	• *Asanas* can be made as simple or as intense as needed per the ability of the seeker. • Reiki raja yogi can send spiritual healing using pure divine grace or pure divine will or using a combination of the two.
Primary Purpose	• Self-healing • Heal the body, aura, chakras, and mind such that holistic happiness is achieved. • Either manifest your desires or dissolve them to achieve happiness.	• Self-realization • Magnetize the chakras through *pranayama* such that they are aligned toward the crown so that self-realization is achieved.		• Both self-healing and self-realization • Self-healing for those who need to heal their life situations, such as health, career, relationships, and so on.

				• The *sadhak* or practitioner develops the power to project the power of the heart and third-eye chakras externally to heal situations or align them toward the crown chakra to experience self-realization.
Experiences during practice	• A mysterious feeling of love and divine intoxication that's relaxing and healing	• An energetic feeling in the spine, which then converts to peace in the no-mind state in the *para avastha* or after-state of meditation • No-mind and no-breath states		• A combination of divine love and divine peace and ultimately a state of absorption, including no-mind and no-breath states—which cannot be described in words.

Deity references	• Radha, Mother Mary	• Shiva • Mahavatar Babaji or Shiv Gorakshnath, Jesus	• Brham, the Absolute • Shree Param Brham, the Absolute in a personalized form
Approach	• Considers the seeker's starting point and provides him or her techniques to fulfill desires to find happiness based on his or her evolution	• Directs everyone to self-realization	• Encourages everyone to self-realize but considers the seeker's starting state and provides tools for healing life situations as well as for self-realization
Chakras healed	• Thirty-three energy points, including major and minor chakras	• Seven major chakras, which in turn are expected to energize the rest of the minor chakras	• Thirty-three energy points, including major and minor chakras

| Empowerment | • Uses symbols to empower the techniques | • Uses mantras in *pranayama* | • Uses mantras that are more powerful than the original Reiki symbols, but easier to practice by seekers worldwide |

CHAPTER 12

A Note about the Guru-Disciple Relationship

* * *

WHY DOES A GURU CHARGE a fee or an energy exchange?

The reason for this is that the barrier of the energy exchange keeps casual seekers away. These are the seekers who just want to try out different things without a serious commitment. The path of Reiki raja-yoga is not for them. It is far more deep and powerful than what is considered suitable for a casual seeker.

It is only for serious seekers who are willing to make an investment of energy—in terms of both money and time.

Another important thing to understand is that the process of energy exchange also keeps those seekers away who have a misconception about how spirituality works. These seekers believe that spirituality and cleansing of karma is free.

This is a misconception that forces people to live agnostic of God's consciousness outside of churches and temples. This means that when they are not in a church or a temple, they are not really worried about whether they are doing good or bad. And when they feel the burden of their bad karma, or go through tough times as a result of the reaction of their bad karma, they quickly run to the temple or the church; they have a feeling that God is there waiting for them to wash out their bad karma and bring them good luck. While that works for a limited period of time, sometimes people become habituated to the process, and instead of being conscious of their actions throughout the day or the week, they just feel that they can do whatever they want to and then they can go to God and fix it; a lot of us do that, even without realizing it.

In both these cases, the concept of energy exchange sends a message across to people that this is an investment. The path of spirituality and yoga is an education—education to transform yourself completely—which includes your transformation of your karma, energy, mind-set, everything. And you must make an investment to do that; you must put some skin in the game.

Why does a spiritual guru charge for giving Reiki treatment and guidance?

A true spiritual guru is someone who has attained a deep realization of the Absolute and can now lead you toward that goal. Gurus help their disciples find their true selves, and in the process attain that oneness with the Absolute. During this journey, an extremely spiritual bond develops between the guru and the disciple.

Whatever is happening in our life—suffering or pleasurable experiences—is a result of either having a karmic debt or having a lot of good karma.

In the case of karmic debt, we owe something back to the universe, and we owe something to other human beings, which maybe we had taken in the past; these human beings include our fellow humans where we were not able to complete the exchange. This imbalance of energy during the process of karmic exchange is what leads to a debt or a credit situation, and healing is a way in which the healer sends positive power to your karmic bank balance to increase the positive karma in your bank balance and dissolve the negative karma. As a result of this, you do incur a karmic debt, especially if the healer is performing a karmic healing, which is a very specific healing where a deep cleansing of your karma is done; hence, when karmic healing is performed, you must pay an energy exchange.

It is not necessary to pay this in the form of money only; it could be in the way of service or some other kind of support. In ancient India, disciples used to go to *gurukuls* (schools run by gurus where people would come to get an education). Unlike today's schools or *ashrams*, in older days, most students would live in the *ashram* and participate in the chores—like going to the forest and bringing firewood, taking care of the animals including cattle, keeping the ashram clean, and performing all sorts of mundane and important jobs. Today that kind of situation does not exist because people are so busy and they do not get an opportunity to balance their karmic exchange.

When there is no energy exchange, the full result of healing is not achieved. In my experience in my healing life as a guru, I have found that healing does not happen properly in case the energy exchange is not proper.

Let me now come to the concept of *guru dakshina*. *Dakshin* means south, and *dakshina* means that which flows toward the south. This word is chosen to represent energy that flows from north to south. The idea is that when a guru comes in contact with you, he or she uplifts you and moves your energies toward the north.

Your lifestyle may be mundane, or you may be suffering; whenever you are disconnected from the ultimate goal of life, which is self-realization, your guru can help in uplifting your energy field in the direction of north. He or she moves your energies from your lower chakras, applies his or her own willpower and grace, taps into the divine grace, and channels that grace into you to uplift that energy and move it toward the north.

This transformation of yourself into a higher plane is being facilitated by your guru. To balance that transformation, you need to move something from north to the south, and in most cases, it is something material, because in the south, the three lower chakras store your energies of wealth, material knowledge, and physical effort.

Therefore, when the guru moves you toward the spiritual north, in order to counterbalance the karmic equation, you also need to move something material toward the guru, toward south. In today's world, sometimes money is the most convenient way because people are short of time, but in reality, *guru dakshina* could be anything; it could be commitment of time for the work of the guru or spreading the message of the guru, or if your finances permit, it could be financial as well.

An important understanding of energy exchange is that nothing in this world is free. As long as we are living, we are bound by karma. There are a few people who become *jeevan mukt*, implying that no new karma is formed on them or creates an impression on them; they are working on this world in a free condition working out their latent karma.

If you are not in the *jeevan mukt* state, you are either in a state of karmic debt or a state of karmic credit, and through healing, you don't want to become more indebted to anybody. It is important to achieve a balance.

It is also possible that when a guru gives you something, he or she forgives you or does not charge you anything. That is only possible in cases where the guru is healing directly through the power of divine grace and is not applying his or her individual willpower. Here again I must caution you that if a guru gives you anything for free, first of all, the guru needs to be clear that he or she will not ask for anything in return; otherwise you may end up in a situation like *Eklavya,* where Guru *Dronacharya* asked for his thumb since he had not given any *dakshina*.

You must also understand that if a guru gives you something for free, God forbid, if this guru experiences a time when he or she is in need of energy, the law of karmic balance will initiate the transfer of energies from the aura of the disciples into the aura of the guru. This will lead to depletion in the energy bodies of the disciples.

There is a popular guru in India who teaches yoga. This guru later got into politics. The moment this happened and the guru ran into some troubled times, a number of his followers started getting sick; this was because all these followers were indebted to this guru. They had not completed their energy exchange because the guru was giving all the techniques for free. And now when the guru was in need, automatically because of the law of nature or the law of karmic balance, the energies without the disciples' knowing were drawn from the aura of the disciples and were being transferred into the aura of the guru. This was causing depletion in the disciples' energy bodies and helping the guru come out of the political challenges that he was facing. So, here you could see that if the karmic exchange is not completed properly, then it creates an uncertainty in the guru-disciple relationship or the healer-healee relationship.

That said, you must be cautious of gurus who are greedy—implying that you must exercise caution in the process of choosing your guru. However, once you have chosen your guru, you have to surrender and respect the law of energy exchange through four things—*samarpan, sadhna, seva,* and *samarthan*.

Samarpan means that you are completely surrendered to the guru—just like *Meera Bai,* who drank poison. In this case, you are one with the guru, and you do not have to pay any energy exchange; your suffering is the guru's suffering, and the guru's suffering is your suffering. Complete surrender is, however, extremely rare.

Sadhna means that you are doing your practice regularly, and your ultimate goal is realization of the Absolute and not healing from sickness, getting a new job or a new car, and so on. Your aim is only the Absolute, and you do not really care about your health or whatever happens to you; you focus only on your *sadhna.* In this case also no energy exchange is required because doing this *sadhna* itself is the biggest energy exchange that you can give to your guru.

Seva is where you perform services in the guru's organization.

Samarthan means that you help the guru spread his or her message; this could be mental support or financial support.

Financial support is often considered most convenient. I have had disciples come to me and tell me that they could not pay for energy exchange during their initiation, and I have offered them to work in my organization for eight to ten hours. In most cases, these people did not show up since they were busy.

If you are unable to devote time and are not willing to pay any other form of energy exchange, and yet expect upliftment, I should warn you that it will result in an imbalanced equation that every guru and healee should avoid. The bottom line is that if you value something in life, you would be willing to pay for it in some way, shape, or fashion (this has also been Mikao Usui's realization in life). A lesson learned from Mikao Usui's life is that when he started healing the beggars on the street without any energy exchange and made them healed whole and complete, within an year he found them come back on the street again because they did not value what was given to them and felt that it was easier for them to beg in the street than to work. The importance of healing is realized when you pay for it in some way.

Mikao Usui has mentioned that there must be an energy exchange—ranging from a thank you or gift of flowers or fruit or whatever *dakshina* that the guru sets for you. The Reiki power is invaluable; you cannot put a cost on God or Reiki power.

The healer or guru typically asks you to pay for any kind of karmic healing that is being done on you and to pay for the time that the healer is spending on you. Time can have different values for different healers and different gurus. All healers should set up the value for their healing for whatever time is worth to them so that they don't become unapproachable. At the same time, it should not be a mass feast kind of a situation where everyone comes for a free meal and doesn't value the healing techniques and doesn't implement the healing that they have received because it came free to them.

Guru dakshina is your way of thanking the guru who has helped you discover your true self. It is again extremely spiritual; it is your way of expressing gratitude toward the Absolute as you become one with him. As you give back to your guru through the process of *guru dakshina*, you also ensure that you are demonstrating your true gratitude for all that you have learned.

Another reason why *guru dakshina* is extremely important is because without complete surrender, it is next to impossible to progress on the spiritual path. Hence, the importance of the physical expression of this surrender.

When disciples give *guru dakshina*, they express their gratitude for all that they have learned during their spiritual journey. We have seen examples of how if the disciples only take stuff and do not give anything in return, they lose what they attained, since they did not attach any value to it. This is the reason why *guru dakshina* must be given with joy; the very act of *dakshina* initiates grace.

CHAPTER 13
Yantras or Instruments of Energy

* * *

THE YANTRA IS AN IMMENSELY powerful and dynamic sacred instrument or symbol or picture that has the potential of energizing your inner as well as the universal life force to its fullest. These instruments have the power to harness universal healing energies to the fullest.

Yantras can enhance the affluence, prosperity, and peace in your house. They can also ensure that you achieve the balance and harmony you are seeking in your personal life and are safeguarded from the evil eye.

Crystals can also be called a type of *yantra*. They are like blank CDs, with some base energy and the ability to store the charge of energy. It is the guru or healer who has to charge (or train) the crystal so that it is fully useful for the healee. This is the same as putting the music of your choice on the CD. A blank CD has limited use, but a CD with music can transform lives.

Some *yantras* offered at the Divine Heart Center are:

BEADS FOR AURA HEALING
These healing beads are made of quartz crystals or *rudraksha* beads, which are programmed to emanate healing energies and help enhance your aura.

The Divine Heart Center healing and protection pendant is made of a natural crystal personally charged by the masters of the Divine Heart Center with the energies of spiritual healing and protection. This is a novel way of making the Reiki power reach seekers everywhere. This can also be called a talisman. The pendant creates energy of protection around the deserving and ethical wearer and also spiritually heals the wearer's body and mind.

Cards for intention healing

These healing cards are programmed using spiritual power to circulate the energies of the specific intention they are made for. Some healing cards can also be customized by the user to heal a specific situation in life.

These cards can be used to invite love and joy into your house or to spiritually heal you of a particular situation.

Vastu healing

Vastu healing is the healing of the space where one lives. This is done using powerful instruments to improve the spiritual and mental energy field of your home, office, shop, and other premises. These are carefully selected by the Divine Heart Center and programmed to give you the maximum benefit by divine and gurus' grace.

These *yantras* use ancient principles of *vastu* and modern science of spiritual and mental energy management. For example, powerful *yantras* can attract and enhance the flow of material energies (e.g., yellow energies) and help in improving the finances of a household or an organization. They can help improve overall abundance. The use of *yantras* can also improve the financial inflows or sales for businesses.

The *yantra* directly interacts with the bioenergy fields (aura) of a person or with the spatial energy (*oorja*) of the premises. It can rectify the deficiency of spiritual and mental energies and can plug leaks in the energy fields that are the cause of the depletion of energies.

CHAPTER 14
Putting It All into Practice

* * *

As a practitioner of Reiki raja-yoga, you must avoid the two extremes of austerity and luxury. You can never achieve perfection in the art and science of Reiki raja-yoga if you eat too much, do not eat at all, sleep too much, do not sleep at all, work too much, or do not work at all.

Once you achieve mastery in Reiki raja-yoga, you are able to burn the enclosure of ignorance that engulfs you. The esoteric vision of nirvana becomes approachable as your knowledge is purified. Reiki raja-yoga leads to the gift of divine grace and the wisdom of the divine will. It is this divine grace and wisdom that helps the yogi.

By practicing Reiki raja-yoga at least once or twice a day, yogis can reach their goal of holistic happiness at a much faster pace. In the ultimate stages of devoted practice, selected yogis discover the ever-expanding joy of self-realization and merge with the Absolute.

Let me ask you a question here. Let us take the case of your eyes. What if I told you that you had two eyes but your eyes did not see? It puts you in doubt, correct? In fact, you are now wondering if this statement "Eyes do not see" makes any sense.

The fact is that there is a brain center in your head; this is what helps you see. If we remove this brain center from your head, your eyes will still be there and you will have the retina; however, you will not be able to process the information that you notice (or what you call "see"). Therefore, you will not be able to see.

You sometimes notice people sleeping with their eyes open. All objects are present in front of these people, yet they are unable to see. The reason for this is because they are able to control the brain center; their eyes are detached from the brain center.

When you see something, the mind takes the impression and presents it to its constructive faculty. This is called the *buddhi*; it is the *buddhi* that reacts and leads to ego.

Your organs or *indriyas* combine together with *manas* or mind, *buddhi*, and *ahamkar* to form the antahkarana or the internal instrument.

The whirlpool of thought in your mind or chitta is termed vritti. If you notice, thoughts are like the repulsive forces in your mind. The chitta may take hold of some forces, absorb them, and repel them as thoughts. Therefore, the mind is not as intelligent as it seems. **It is the soul behind the mind that is intelligent.**

The mind is only an instrument in the hands of the soul.

Try looking at the bottom of the lake. Can you see that? You will only be able to catch a glimpse, and that only when the ripples have subsided and the water is calm. You will never be able to view the bottom if the water is muddy and full of dirt. However, if the water is clear, you will be able to look at and admire the bottom.

If I were to analyze this situation, I would say that the bottom of the lake is your own true self, the waves in the lake are your vrittis, and the lake in itself is the chitta.

The chitta can have three states: the natural pure state or the *sattva*, where you experience serenity and calmness; the second active state called the *rajas*, where your ultimate motive is enjoyment and power; and the third stage of darkness or *tamas*, where your ultimate motive is to injure and harm others.

By nature, the chitta always tries to get back into its natural state, and the path of Reiki raja-yoga helps it along the way. There are four forms in which the chitta can manifest itself:

The first form is the form where it tries to get into activity. This is the scattering form. The second form is where it tries to get into the injury mode; this is termed the dullness form. The third form comes naturally to the *devas* and other sacred people and is termed as the gathering form—when it tries to gather its attention toward its center. The last or the fourth form is when it tries to concentrate, and this is what leads you to *samadhi*.

Just like the lake, when your mind is calm, you are able to concentrate and be your true self. This is the stage when you would have achieved your ultimate motive—holistic happiness! This is the stage that will lead to unison with the Absolute and you will achieve absolute self-realization.

This can only be achieved through practice. You must practice every day in order to ensure that your mind is restrained in chitta form and is not impacted by the waves.

Your first spiritual goal is to perceive the soul itself. Most ignorant individuals view their bodies as their soul. Some learned ones view their mind as their souls. However, both these are mistaken. A number of waves are present in the chitta. A few of them may rise, and you may perceive these as covering the soul or maybe see a little reflection of the soul through these waves. So, if you observe a wave of anger, you perceive your soul to be angry. You begin to say, "I am angry." These are your samskaras engulfing the soul.

You cannot feel the real nature of the soul until there is just one wave in your chitta. Reiki raja-yoga can teach you to make that one wave so strong that all other waves simply disappear.

And through practice, you are also able to even suppress that single wave. This leads to *samadhi* or seedlessness. Now the soul can be felt in its own glory; it is neither born, nor does it dies. It just directs you to be one with that Absolute.

One of the things that I would like to leave you with, a gurumantra, is to think deeply and determine what is the ultimate goal of your life that you are seeking, what is the purpose of your life, and where would you want to direct this life.

What is the *paramarth* of your life (*param* means ultimate, and *arth* means meaning)?

And now it is the time to decide. After reading this book, you should be able to decide if the practices of Reiki raja-yoga can support you in achieving your ultimate goal. If you are clear about your goal and if you are determined to make the self-effort as well as be surrendered to the higher power of the Absolute, you will realize that everything else in your life starts aligning, everything falls into place, and the universe begins to help you. All the pieces of the puzzle suddenly seem to align together now only to help you achieve your goal.

Through this book, you have understood why you would need healing through Reiki power. You have also understood that your complete personality is not just your physical body, but also the energy system that keeps it running, your emotional body, your mental body, and your spiritual body. You now know how your chakras are able to pump this energy throughout your body and how the blocks in these chakras impact you. The overactive or underperforming chakras impact you both in terms of your behavior and the things that you experience in life.

You have also understood the power of healing through Reiki raja-yoga, where Reiki is *para* shakti—beyond energies; it is the power of love, and it attracts all the energy that is needed to heal a particular point. The power of will or the kundalini *(param)* shakti is generated by the *pranayamas* and the eight steps of the raja-yoga tradition. Through the book, I have tried to explain how the *para* shakti and kundalini shakti come together to create this unique approach for realizing holistic happiness, which in turn leads you deeper into self-realization.

I hope that you will be able to see the applicability of the path of Reiki raja-yoga in your life. This path has been taught to me by my gurus and then refined by me under the guidance of the Absolute directly.

From time to time, I check with the Absolute if what we are teaching and how we are teaching is accurate, advantageous, and beneficial to whoever is going to learn, especially in these modern times.

Now, wherever you are in life, wherever you are in the practice of unfoldment, you will see that the practice of Reiki raja-yoga will take you to the next level. You could be at a point where your immediate need is to be free of some chronic experience or to find relief after a bad relationship or experience or to tackle something at work that may not be going in the right direction; you may be at a point where you are completely stressed about life, and you have taken all practical steps to eradicate that stress. However, you still feel that even after taking all measures, putting forth all your efforts, there is something else that requires to be done; there is something else that is missing and could give you the correct outcome in life. And that's where the philosophy and practice of Reiki and raja-yoga will help you.

You could also be at a point where you could have everything in life. You have health, wealth, and relationships; you are experienced; you are a world traveler; and you have wisdom—but you still feel the need to find the Absolute. And the other end of the spectrum of Reiki raja-yoga can help you get into the deeper stages of *samadhi* and to find your oneness with the Absolute.

Such a versatile flexible philosophy, which is also authentic, which simplifies the esoteric teachings of the ancient times into something that you can understand, is very rare to find. This technique of Reiki raja-yoga is a royal gem—the gem of love.

Reiki raja-yoga is an all-inclusive, nondenominational path, designed for the busy person but also for a very sincere person who is not looking to escape from reality. This person is capable of facing reality but wants additional help to realize his or her full potential. He or she wants to realize his or her complete personality right from his or her conscious mind to his or her soul—and those are the people who benefit from this path.

I hope you are one of these people, and after you finish reading this book, I hope you practice these meditations and come to an informed conclusion that this is the path that is right for you, which can start, accelerate, or balance your journey toward holistic happiness and also take you toward self-realization.

In this book, I have presented many ideas that are abstract. However, I have tried to present these abstract ideas in words. Whenever you present something that is abstract or infinite into words, there is a chance that some impurities may also be present. One adulteration is the limits of the language in which that abstract idea has been described; another impurity is the guru's ability to channel the idea precisely or put it in words due to his or her own mastery of the language.

If there has been any plus or minus in this text, I apologize to the Absolute. The purpose of this text is to encourage you to take action and seek real experience through practice and not through theory. Unless you experience for yourself what I have tried to teach you through this book and feel the profound truth that I have revealed to you, everything will just become theory.

So, practice, practice, and practice. I encourage you to experience it yourself through practice.

GLOSSARY

- Agyan: ignorance
- Ahamkar: the I-principle, self-conceit or egoism
- Ahimsa: non-harming or noninjury, the single most important moral discipline
- Akash: space
- Ananda: the state of pure bliss
- Asana: a physical posture in the practice of yoga
- Atman: the transcendental self (our true nature or identity)
- Aum: Similar to the Latin word *omne*, the Sanskrit word *aum* means "all" and conveys concepts of omnipresence
- Avadhoot: a renouncer who often engages in unconventional behavior
- Avatar: a manifestation of God in an earthly form (usually in the form of a human or an animal)
- Avidya: ignorance
- Ayurveda: one of India's ancient systems of medicine
- *Bhagavad Gita*: the oldest full-fledged yoga book that contains teachings of karma yoga, samkhya yoga, and bhakti yoga
- Bhajans: Hindu devotional songs
- Bhakta: devotee
- Bhakti: devotion or love
- Bhrama: delusion
- Brahm: the ultimate reality or the Absolute
- Buddhi: understanding, wisdom, intellect, or the higher mind or the seat of wisdom
- Chitta or chit: feeling, unbroken awareness of consciousness; subconscious mind
- Dargah: the shrine or tomb of a Muslim saint
- Deva: a male deity such as Lord Shiva
- Devi: A female deity such as Ma Kali
- Devta: conscious being

- Dham: abode, a place for pilgrimage
- Dharana: concentration
- Dharma: the righteous way of living
- Dhyana: meditation
- Dronacharya: the royal preceptor and master of military arts in the epic *Mahabharata*
- Eklavya: a prince in the epic *Mahabharata* who had to give his thumb as his due to his guru
- Guna: three primary qualities of nature or of human character
- Guru: a spiritual teacher; from the Sanskrit root *gru* meaning "having gravity"; also, dispeller of darkness from *gu* meaning darkness and *ru* meaning dispeller
- Gurumantra: mantra that has been initiated by the guru
- Jagat: world
- Japa: the recitation of mantras
- Jivanmukta: one who is liberated while alive
- Jivatman: the individual consciousness
- Kali: a goddess signifying a wild and destructive character
- Krishna: a Hindu deity recognized as the supreme God and the eighth incarnation of Lord Vishnu
- Lakshmana: the younger brother of Lord Rama
- Loo: hot and dry winds
- Lord Hanuman: a deity worshipped in India
- Rama: the seventh avatar of Vishnu
- Lord Vishnu: the supreme God in Hinduism; one who is present everywhere
- Mahavir: the greatest warrior
- Manas or mana: the lower mind, which is bound to senses and processes information
- Mantra: a sacred phrase or sound that leads to a transformative impact on the mind of the person through recitation
- Maya: cosmic hypnosis; illusion by which the world is seen as separate from the ultimate reality

- Meera Bai: a sixteenth-century Hindu mystic who remained unharmed by the poison given to her due to her devotion to Lord Krishna
- Nadis: energy channels inside the body
- Para: beyond
- Param-atman: the ultimate self
- Pir: a spiritual guide or a Sufi master
- Radha: name of the divine mother or Godman Krishna's spouse
- *Ramayana*: an epic depicting the story of Lord Rama
- Rishi: sage
- Sadhna: the disciplined practice of learning
- Samskara: mental impression; value
- Sankalpa: limiting concept
- Sat: eternal consciousness or the ultimate reality
- Shakti: will
- Shiva: the Divine or a deity
- Shree Param Brham: the Absolute in a personalized form
- Stuti: praise or glorification
- Sukshma: subtle
- Teej: festival celebrated in northern India to welcome the monsoon season
- *Vedas*: the oldest collection of Hindu sacred texts
- Vrat: fast
- Vritti: proclivities or thoughts

Made in the USA
Middletown, DE
22 October 2015